Untold Stories of Polish Heroes from World War II

Aleksandra Ziolkowska-Boehm

FOREWORD BY JAMES S. PULA

For Marcia Wolnicki

with all my good wishes,

Aleksandra

Feb 18, 2018

Hamilton Books

Lanham • Boulder • New York • Toronto • Plymouth, UK

Copyright © 2018 by Hamilton Books
4501 Forbes Boulevard, Suite 200, Lanham, Maryland 20706
Hamilton Books Acquisitions Department (301) 459-3366

Unit A, Whitacre Mews, 26-34 Stannary Street,
London SE11 4AB, United Kingdom

Library of Congress Control Number: 2017951808
ISBN: 978-0-7618-6983-2 (pbk : alk. paper)—ISBN: 978-0-7618-6984-9 (electronic)

Cover photos: (Left) Rudolf S. Falkowski. Mustang IV Sqd. 303. Photo from the archives of and used by permission of Stefan Władysiuk. (Top right) Warsaw Rising 1944. Wieslaw Chrzanowski from the archives of and used by permission of Marta Chrzanowska-Ławniczak. (Bottom right) Wieslaw Chrzanowski from the archives of and used by permission of Marta Chrzanowska-Ławniczak.

In memory of my beloved parents,
Antonina and Henryk Ziolkowski

Contents

Foreword   vii
James S. Pula, Purdue University

Preface   xi

Acknowledgments   xv

1   Father and Son: Tadeusz and Zbigniew Brzeziński   1

2   Two Great Passions— Flying and Writing: Rudolf S. Falkowski   27

3   "I carried the films on my head" Photographer of the Warsaw
Uprising: Wiesław Chrzanowski   45

4   Varsovians in the States: Krystyna and Marek Jaroszewicz   61

5   "I was that child about to be born...": Maria Kowal   85

6   The Child from Bialowieza Primeval Forest, the Urals, Isfahan
and Mexico: Danuta Batorska   93

7   Captive of the Theatre: Marion Andre   101

8   Angola-Born, Brazil-Based Poet, Artist: Tomasz Lychowski   117

Annex: Literary Journalism, Storytelling, or Literature of Fact   125

Index   139

About the Author   145

Foreword

James S. Pula, Purdue University

The eminent historian Thomas Carlyle, in his essay "On History" published in 1830, asserted that "Social Life is the aggregate of all the individual men's Lives who constitute society; History is the essence of innumerable biographies." While we might more properly say it is the sum of *all* people's lives, not just men's, Carlyle's statement is a fundamental truth of the historical profession. History is, after all, not the accumulation of names and dates and recitations of what happened, it is an attempt to study people, how they behave, and why they make the decisions they do. It is an attempt to study how people interact in groups, what motivates them, and how their behaviour is influenced by both their own personal experiences and the external forces that act upon them. It is, in the final analysis, an attempt to understand the cause and effect relationships that form the chain of the human chronicle over time.

Carlyle also stated, in a subsequent publication, that "The history of the world is but the biography of great men." Indeed, most often those who write biography have chosen to concentrate their efforts on "great men" or "great women" precisely in the belief that the progression of history depended, as Carlyle suggested, on the decisions of these "heroes." Despite the fact that Herbert Spencer began challenging this idea as early as the 1860s, arguing instead that these "great men" were simply products of the social environments in which they lived, the so-called "Great Man Theory" was prominent among professional historians until after World War II when post-war scholars began to delve more deeply into social history.

Regardless of which of these theories one subscribes to, it should be clear that a full understanding of the historical process must include studies of the social and economic conditions of societies as well as biographies of the people on which a clear understanding of history is based—but not just the "great" people. Biographies of "average" individuals who exist in a society, have their own experiences and are acted upon by their surrounding environments, are essential to a clear and complete understanding of the past and its influence on the present. In this respect, Aleksandra Ziołkowska-Boehm has made a major contribution to furthering the understanding of World War II, and especially the part played by Poland and Poles, with her compilation of individual biographies of people who participated in many of its formative events.

Ziołkowska-Boehm's protagonists include a variety of people and experiences that enhance the usefulness of the volume—Tadeusz Brzeziński, a member of the Polish diplomatic corps who was on assignment in Canada at the outbreak of the war and went on to serve as Consul General for the Polish Government-in-Exile in London; Rudolf S. Falkowski, a freshly minted pilot who escaped from the Soviet Union to fly fighters over Great Britain; Wiesław Chrzanowski who became a photographer of the Warsaw Uprising; Krystyna Brzezicka and Marek Jaroszewicz grew up in Warsaw where she served as a nurse during the Warsaw Uprising and he escaped to France before being interned in Switzerland; Maria Kowal was actually born while her parents were fleeing during the war, so her personal memories are of her post-war era move to the United States; Danuta Batorska who grew up in the Białowieża Forest before she was forcefully deported with her family to the Soviet Urals, later escaping to the Middle East and eventually Mexico; Marion Andre who escaped the Lwów ghetto to fight in the Warsaw Uprising and later founded a theatre group in Montréal; and Tomasz Łychowski who, though only eight when the war began, but survived Pawiak Prison, moved to Brazil, and became an internationally-known poet and artist.

Tadeusz Brzeziński had already achieved status and an upper-class lifestyle when he arrived as a member of the Polish diplomatic corps to his new assignment in Canada in 1938. Born of Polish parents in the Austro-Hungarian Empire, he enjoyed the advantages of study in Vienna, The Hague and Lwów where he received a doctorate in law and political science in 1919. The essay on Brzeziński includes valuable information on his attempts, while posted in Leipzig in the 1930s, to protest Nazi treatment of the Jews and to actively help them to escape by providing necessary documents. It also records his wartime services and post-war activities, providing original source materials of particular interest to researchers. The experiences of the father are well-complemented by the briefer commentary on his son, Zbigniew, who rose to prominence as the U.S. National Security Advisor under President Jimmy Carter. The younger Brzeziński's recollections supplement his fathers, but also add his own observations of family life in the wartime and immediate post-war eras.

Rudolf Falkowski dreamed of flying as a young elementary school student when he also began keeping a journal of his experiences. The first passion would thrust him into the maelstrom of aerial combat, while the latter would lead to publication of his first book at age 88. Born into a family of modest means, he had difficulties in school but managed to enrol in a pilot training program which he completed in the summer of 1939 on the eve of the German invasion. Following the Sikorski-Majski Agreement in 1941 he managed to travel to Great Britain where his knowledge of flying earned him a pilot's wings flying fighters. The author's treatment of him includes lengthy quotations from his journal and their correspondence that provide valuable historical information of the times he lived through, as well as his own persona.

Wiesław Chrzanowski was born in Sosnowiec but grew up in Gdańsk where his father obtained a job in the shipyard until the family moved to Warsaw in 1930. His childhood appears to have been typical both in education and his enjoyment of sports. In 1939 he served in the defense of the fortress at Modlin, then joined the underground. With the beginning of the Warsaw Uprising, Chrzanowski determined to record the experiences of his unit. Some of his photographs appear in an album prepared by the Warsaw Uprising Museum, while others have appeared on Polish postage stamps. His work, numbering over 200 images and accompanying documentary text, forms a unique and irreplaceable historical record of virtually every aspect of his unit's part in the Uprising, the people who defied the Germans for 63 brutal days, and his experiences in captivity.

Krystyna and Marek Jaroszewicz were born in Warsaw, knew each other while growing up, but were separated by the war. Krystyna shared with the author memories of her childhood including a beautiful manor house in Gulbiny and visits to the eastern borderlands, as well as the painful experiences under the German occupation. During the war Krystyna served as a nurse during the Warsaw Uprising, providing her recollections of this and a post-war refugee camp in Switzerland. Marek's father was a chemist and a prominent supporter of Józef Piłsudski, perhaps a little better situated economically and socially than most of the other protagonists who appear in the book. He was to enter Warsaw University of Technology to study architecture in the fall of 1939, but the invasion intervened. Joining the Polish armed forces, he escaped to the West but was interned in Switzerland with the fall of France. The two reconnected in Zurich and married in 1945. In addition to the wartime experiences, the dual-biography presents first-hand reflections on the experiences of refugees on arrival in the post-war United States.

Maria Kowal was from a small village in Volhynia. Her family had to escape from Ukrainian nationalists during the war and she was actually born in a church in 1943 during their flight. The family was eventually taken as laborers to Germany. Maria recalled as a young girl their post-war move to the United States and her experiences growing to maturity. Danuta Batorska was the daughter of a forestry administrator in the Białowieża Forest. With the war the family was forcibly relocated to the Urals when Danuta was only four. Later, she was evacuated to Teheran following the formation of General Władysław Anders's army. From the Middle East, in the post-war years she went to the Santa Rosa resettlement center in Mexico. Her memories of the NKVD arrest, the forced exile, the journey to Teheran, and finally the Santa Rosa colony and her eventual settling down in the United States.

Marion Andre, the son of Emil and Roza Tenenbaum who were both pharmacists by trade, was born in France while his parents were briefly there, but raised in the Lwów area. His introduction to World War II was to see his English teacher shot and killed by a German as he walked down the street holding a book. Forced into the ghetto, he and his mother managed to escape but his sister and father became victims of German atrocities. After fighting in the Warsaw Uprising in 1944 he was imprisoned, but following the war migrated to Canada where he began a literary career basing his early work on his own experiences. He also established a theatre group in Montréal where he produced plays and passed on his knowledge to students.

Tomasz Łychowski was somewhat unique from birth: the son of a lawyer from Kiev and a German mother, he came into the world in the Portuguese African colony of Angola in 1934. Returning to Poland in time for the outbreak of the war, his parents became active members of the underground until the entire family was betrayed and sent to Pawiak Prison. Amazingly, all three survived the horrors of imprisonment including his father Tadeusz who was sent to Auschwitz. Following the war the family reunited and began a new life in Brazil. Tomasz became an internationally-known poet and artist, publishing books of poetry in Portuguese, English, and Polish.

A strength of the volume is the variety of its protagonists—their ages and backgrounds are all different, they had different experiences, and they include the experiences of civilians and women, both of which deserve more treatment in the historical literature. Her handling of characters brings them to life, gives them personality, establishes a connection with the reader. Each of these is individually important in its own right. Yet, at the same time, the breadth of their collective experiences paints a broad picture of the many divergent encounters the war triggered. It is this very breadth that makes it more valuable in understanding the scope of wartime events and their effect on the people who lived through them.

Preface

The generation of people who survived the Second World War is almost gone. As Tom Brokaw said, they were a very special kind of people: brave, patriotic in a way that now is almost "unfashionable". The men who saw action in the war were unquestionably brave, as were those who endured their fate and did their best, sometimes—their best meant survival.

My eight narratives presented in this book deal with Polish destinies, untold stories of people, mostly very young, who survived the Second World War, and how great an impact the war had on their lives.

In 1939, both Germany (September 1st) and Soviet Union (September 17) invaded a partitioned Poland. They launched a horrific occupation designed to destroy the country and its people. Particularly Polish leaders and the intelligentsia were arrested and many executed. The German occupation and atrocities in Poland generally are well known. Not so well known forms of atrocities are that if a German soldier was killed by the Polish underground, 100 Polish citizens randomly selected were executed. Poland was the only Nazi-occupied country where saving Jews carried the death penalty. If a Polish citizen aided a Jew by hiding, helping or feeding him, he was subject to execution along with his entire family. [1]

The Soviet occupation is less well known than German actions. The NKVD[2] murders of the Polish officers in the Katyn Forest are only one episode in the dismal history of Russian atrocities. Around 1.5 million Polish were deported into Siberia, another 0.5 million Polish prisoners of war were held in Soviet camps.

The Russian policy changed after the Germans invaded the Soviet Union in June 1941. Hitler launched military operation Barbarossa and reported the victories. Stalin, who moved the Red Army west to annex eastern Poland, faced a new reality. He needed allies. The two most important were Britain that had a treaty with Poland, and America, that had a large number of citizens of Polish ancestry who were appalled by the German and Soviet invasions. Foreign Secretary Anthony Eden, Churchill's deputy, encouraged the Polish Prime Minister in Exile, military and political leader General Władysław Sikorski to approach the Soviets. Sikorski opened negotiations with Ivan Majski, the Soviet ambassador to London. General Sikorski became the architect of the resulting agreement, sometimes called the Sikorski-Majski Agreement. Basically, the Soviets granted "amnesty" to many Polish citizens. On August 12, 1941, Stalin released interned Poles offering them two alternatives: they could fight together with the Red Army or leave through Iran and join the Polish forces fighting with the Western Allies. A small number of civilians were allowed to accompany them. As a result, some 18,000 Polish children reached Iran. Many were orphaned, and some had become separated from their parents.

General Władysław Anders organized a 40,000-man army which fought with the British 8th army. Known as the Polish II Corps, they fought in North Africa and in Italy. One of their most important battles was at Monte Casino[3] that became a legend in Polish history. In the cemetery, there are graves of 1072 soldiers—beside Polish, there are Byelorussians, Ukrainians and Jewish—all released and taken by General Anders from the Soviet Union.

When the war ended, on June 8, 1946, to honor British servicemen as well as allies that fought together with Britain, Prime Minister Clement Attlee organized the London victory parade. Poles who fought with the British were shocked when they were not allowed to march. Prime Minister Clement was concerned about offending Joseph Stalin. The British did invite RAF 303 Squadron made up of Polish pilots who had fought in the Battle of Britain, but were surprised by the Squadron reaction. The RAF 303 Squadron declined to march in the victory parade because their Polish fellow fighters were excluded.

The first story is that of the Polish diplomat, Tadeusz Brzezinski; it relates his actions as a consul in Leipzig during 1931-1935, and later his public services in Montreal. T. Brzezinski's experience as Consul in Leipzig is an informative precursor to the war.

His son, Zbigniew Brzezinski, shares his views on Poland, his country of origin, on Canada where he was educated, and on the United States where he became the National Security Advisor in President Carter's administration. This is the highest political position attainable by a person born outside of the United States.

My second story is about a pilot of the famous 303 Squadron of the RAF. Is shows his love for flying and for books. After the WWII started, he had to join the Red Army.

In two other stories, I show heroes who participated in and survived the Warsaw Rising 1944 and imprisonment in the German concentration camp at Ravensbruck.

The fifth story describes the massacres of Poles in Volhynia and Eastern Galicia (Polish: *rzeź wołyńska*, literally:*Volhynian slaughter*) that were part of an ethnic cleansing operation carried out in Nazi German-occupied Poland by the Ukrainian Insurgent Army (UPA)'s North Command.

The sixth story is told by a mother and daughter, both survivors of deportation to Siberia who following immigration in 1960, have lived in the USA.

The other chapter is dedicated to Marion Andre and his recollections about his ghetto escape, fighting in the 1944 Warsaw Rising, immigration to Canada.

The last story is about most likely the youngest surviving prisoner of Pawiak prison (part of the German concentration death camp in Warsaw) who lives now in Brazil.

In Annex I write how I look at "creative nonfiction", and about my dealing with "real people stories". I stress the importance of gaining trust, of always being ethical with him or her, and to not seek sensationalism in relating the subject's story.

NOTES

1. At Yad Vashem Memorial in Israel there are over six thousand trees memorializing Poles who saved Jews during the Holocaust.

2. NKVD—the People's Commissariat for Internal Affairs (Russiam: Narodnyi Komissariat Vnutrennikh Del), was a law enforcement agency of the Soviet Union that was closely associated with the Soviet secret police, which at times was part of the agency, and is known for its political repression during the era of Joseph Stalin. (See: footnote No. 3: Chapter 6: "The Child from Bialowieza Primeval Forest, the Urals, Isfahan and Mexico -Danuta Batorska").

3. A well know book by Melchior Wańkowicz: "Bitwa o Monte Cassino" (Battle of Monte Cassino), first edition 3 volumes Rome –Milano 1945-47; the latest edition: Warsaw 2009.

Acknowledgments

All the profiles in this volume describe real people and actual events. Their stories are drawn from personal conversations.

I would like to express my special thanks to people who trusted me to share their stories: Danuta Batorska, Maria Kowal, Tomasz Lychowski, and to the late: Marion Andre, Tadeusz and Zbigniew Brzezinski, Halina and Wiesław Chrzanowski, Rudolf S. Falkowski, Krystyna and Marek Jaroszewicz.

I want also to acknowledge my gratitude to Anna Bernat, Bohdan Bułhak, Marta Chrzanowska-Ławniczak, Janusz Dukszta, Jesse Flis, Agnieszka Gernand, Bruce E. Johansen, Grace Kopec, Janusz and Danuta Krasicki, Charles S. Kraszewski, Mariola Marcinkiewicz, Janusz M. Paluch, Mirosława Pałaszewska, Neal Pease, Gosia Porwit, Mira Puacz, James S. Pula, Alla Roylance, Wojtek Stelmaszynski, Ewa Thompson, Thomas Tomczyk, Audrey Ronning Topping, Stefan Władysiuk, Tomasz Wojtkowski, Angela Zubrzycki. I am grateful to Holly Buchanan and Beverly Shellem for their endeavors throughout the publication process.

Many thanks also go to my beloved husband Norman, for his help and support. Norman passed away before the book was published. I am indebted for life for his encouragement and belief in me.

Chapter One

Father and Son

Tadeusz and Zbigniew Brzeziński [1]

Tadeusz Brzeziński did not leave Poland with plans to settle permanently abroad, but arrived in Canada in 1938 as a member of the Polish diplomatic corps. During the Second World War, he served as Consul General for the Polish Government in Exile.

After the war, he decided to remain in Canada.

Tadeusz Brzeziński son of Kazimierz [2] was born in Zloczow on February 21, 1896, Zloczow then being in the Austro-Hungarian Empire. The town was in the part of Poland ceded to the Soviet Union in 1945 and is now Zolochev, in the Ukraine.

Tadeusz completed high school in 1914 and went on to study at universities in Vienna, The Hague and Lwów. In 1919, he graduated from the University of Lwów with a Doctorate in Law and Political Science. Following his studies, he worked for the Galician Credit Society. From 1918 to 1921, he was a soldier with the Polish Army and saw action during the Polish-Russian war. In 1921, he began working for the Public Prosecutor's Office of the Polish Government in Warsaw. That same year, he joined the diplomatic corps, accepting successive posts in Wetphalia and Nadrin, southern Belgium, Saxony and Thuringie, Germany, Ukraine and Canada.

From 1921 to 1922, he was at Westphalia and Nadrin. During this period, immigrant Polish miners were once again taking out Polish citizenship and returning to the re-instated Polish state; or they were moving to France, which had again opened its borders to a wave of Polish immigration.

During the years 1928-1931, Tadeusz headed consular activities at Lille, France. At the time, there were thousands of miners from Poland and Westphalia working in northern France.

From 1931-1935, Brzeziński was the consul at Leipzig, handling the affairs of Polish workers throughout the province of Saxony. The first instances of persecution of the Jews in Germany under Hitler occurred during these years. Brzeziński was instrumental in saving the lives of thousands of Polish Jews, issuing letters, diplomatic notes and petitions in their defense. His name is recorded in the Palestinian Roll of Honor.

Forty-five years later—in 1977—then Israeli Prime Minister Menachem Begin visited U. S. national security advisor Zbigniew Brzeziński, bringing with him letters written in 1933 by Zbigniew's father, Tadeusz Brzeziński. The first letter was dated March 21, 1933—less than two months after Hitler became chancellor of Germany. The letter protested the abuse and destruction of possessions belonging to Jews living in Altenburg.

On April 1, 1933, Hitler announced a boycott of all Jewish businesses. " . . . Looking back now, I suppose what caught us off guard, was how quickly events moved: First with discrimination, then boycotting, then signs of "Jude" across storefronts, and Nazis in brown uniforms watching everyone who walked in . . . " recalled Brzeziński during an interview with the "Montreal Star" (August 23, 1977).

A second letter, dated August 30, 1933, and addressed to the "Saxon Ministry of the Interior," constituted a "complaint of alleged ill-treatment of a number of Polish Jews." The reply stated in part that: "Jews were in protective custody after they had been attacked in 'nationalistic manifestations',"and went on to label the protest as an example of "tightly-interlaced international Jewry."

Menachem Begin sent Tadeusz Brzeziński a letter on August 23, 1977, in which he wrote:

My friend, Dr. Ben-Elissar, who is now the Director of the Prime Minister's Office, carried out a research of the thirties in Europe on a scientific basis and it is due to him that the important documents, written and signed by you, have been found. The Jewish people, dear Mr. Brzeziński, never forget a friend. We are all deeply grateful to you—and forever (. . .)

Thank you for all you did to help my brethren in those dark days, when so few stood with them in their indescribable plight.

With my warmest wishes,
Sincerely yours, M. Begin"

After his tenure in Germany, Brzeziński was appointed to Kharkov, in the Ukraine, where he remained from 1936 to 1937. His next, and last, diplomatic posting was to Canada.

Tadeusz and Leonia[3] Brzeziński, together with their four sons [Zbigniew, Lech, Adam, Jerzy Zylinski], a tutor, a housekeeper, a governess and their pet German shepherd arrived in New York aboard the "Batory." From there, they travelled by train to Montreal. On October 27, 1938, they were met at the Windsor Station in Montreal by the Mayor of the City of Montreal, the consular staff, and representatives of the Polish community. Tadeusz Brzeziński officially took over his diplomatic duties on November 1, 1938.

The Polish Consulate in Montreal had been in existence since November 1, 1919. In 1920, a similar posting was established in Winnipeg. In 1933, a consulate was opened in Ottawa to facilitate direct contact with the Federal Government. (During the war, this office became a mission of the Polish Nation). All the consular offices established by the newly independent Poland were for the benefit of the growing Polish immigrant population in Canada. Re-immigration back to free Poland was minimal; however, during the twenty-year inter war period, the number of Polish immigrants to Canada grew to 160,000.

The consulates—open, visible symbols of the Polish Nation in Canada—undoubtedly helped in the formation of a sense of Polish community spirit. This harmony was heightened during the Second World War, when the threat to and tragedy of the Polish nation brought the immigrants even closer together in common concern for their loved ones and for the nation itself.

The consulate in Montreal served five provinces: Quebec, Ontario, New Brunswick, Nova Scotia and Prince Edward Island.

These provinces had a surface area equal to almost half of Europe. Canada, a country much larger than the U. S., did not as yet have its own long-term immigration policies. It did, however, have regulations which seemed to favor English-speaking immigrants. In 1938, the entire Canadian population numbered only 11 million.

Beyond the standard consular, trade and information activities of any diplomatic posting, the consulate in Montreal also provided what it called "cultural care" for Polish immigrants. In Poland, the Immigration Office in Warsaw handled this function. The main reasons given for moving abroad were overpopulation and poverty in the villages.

Within the consular division of the Ministry of Foreign Affairs in Warsaw, there was an Advisory Committee made up of representatives of the Ministry, the Immigration Office and the Ministry of Education. The Committee started the first records on Poles living abroad and assisted in several projects of a cultural—educational nature. Tadeusz Brzeziński was an active member of this Committee, particularly in coordinating work and in attempting to bring all Poles abroad closer together. His thoughts on establishing the "World Organization of Poles Abroad" were published in the Warsaw Immigrant Quarterly.

The project was not well received in Canada. First, the Polish population was not as great there as it was elsewhere. Also, for a project generated in the homeland, there was not much enthusiasm, which, naturally, was not the idea of the Polish immigrants themselves. In Winnipeg, there was already a Federation of Polish Associations in Canada. A similar Federation was established in Montreal: however, several Polonia organizations, notably the Polish Alliance of Canada and the Polish Association in Winnipeg did not join these umbrella groups.

In 1934, "Swiatpol," an organization for Poles abroad was established. Its future would have been promising, had not the worsening situation in Europe cut short its development.

As soon as Brzeziński took over as consul in Montreal, he contacted the five provincial leaders, the mayors of all the large cities, representatives of the press and radio, the army, various religious organizations and trade and cultural institutions. He personally visited small and large Polish communities in Toronto, Hamilton, Windsor, Kitchener, Wilno, Barry's Bay, Round Lake, Brandford, St. Catharines, London, Oshawa, Kirkland Lake, Timmins, Sudbury, Sherbrooke, Delhi, Chatham and Sault Ste. Marie.

Brzeziński was instrumental in reviving the circulation of the organ of "Związkowiec" (The Alliancer), the newspaper of the Polish Alliance of Canada. In 1937, the paper had been banned in Poland for its alleged radical stance and outspoken criticism of the Polish government. The Polish Alliance was very grateful to Brzeziński for his part in the paper's re-establishment.

Because of increasing anxiety in Europe and the growing threat to Poland, there arose a need to keep public opinion in Canada well-informed and abreast of the latest news. Both the ethnic and Canadian media were concerned about Poland's position. Brzeziński granted many interviews, made several public appearances, and in a large part influenced the positive reaction of Canadians to the threatened nation. Liberal Prime Minister Mackenzie King was a very popular figure among Canadian Poles, as was M. P. Arthur Roebuck, who represented the heavily ethnic riding of Trinity in downtown Toronto.

The outbreak of the Second World War only increased public interest in Poland. Many Polish and Canadian demonstrations were held across the country in support of the Polish cause. Poland was always in the headlines of press and radio news reports. Sometimes demonstrations were even held in localities where there was no Polish population. In March 1940, there was a huge rally in Quebec City, in which government representatives, members of parliament, city officials, university leaders, and many members of the local population participated. The demonstration was led by the Canadian Primate, who urged all Canadians to pray for Poland.

In Charlottetown, Prince Edward Island, there was a rally headed by the Lieutenant Governor, the Premier and the Federal Minister of Defense.

Several assistance campaigns were initiated for Poland and the Polish people: money and relief parcels were sent not only to relatives, but to camp internees and families who had been deported to Germany and the Soviet

Union. Clothing, food and medicine were donated by the Canadian Red Cross, the Canadian Friends of Poland and similar groups. The Red Cross calculated in 1947 that it had shipped equipment and goods to Poland during the war years valued at over $7 million.

In 1940, the second year of the war, the first group of Polish families began arriving in Canada from Western Europe. The Canadian Polish community helped them settle and find employment.

Constant contact was maintained with the Polish Government in Exile, it initially located in France, then later in London. Representatives of the government travelled to Canada to participate in demonstrations and encourage enlistment of relief volunteers in the Polish Army.

The opening of Polish Army Headquarters, together with a recruiting information campaign, brought in the first volunteers, among them Brzezinski's stepson, Jerzy Żyliński. However, the results were not as favorable as anticipated. There were a number of reasons for this: first, the great interest shown at the beginning of the war, later abated. Second, the Polish Government in London approved a Canadian proposal that Canadian citizens of Polish descent should enlist in the Canadian army. Third, once the U. S. entered the war, the number of Polish American volunteers dropped drastically. Pay and family benefits were much greater in the Canadian and U. S. armies, a fact which certainly influenced the recruits' decisions.

In early 1943, the Polish Army Mission in Canada was closed. Volunteers from the Canadian and U. S. received their training in Scotland, then saw action in France, and Holland, and took part in flights over Germany, and in other campaigns.

In 1941, the Polish Government in Exile reached an agreement with Canada whereby Canada would accept several hundred Polish engineers stranded in unoccupied France, to work in the developing Canadian war industry. Polish engineers also came to Canada via Portugal. The newcomers, in gratitude to the Canadian-Polish community for its help, organized special courses in Montreal and Toronto so local Polish Canadians could raise their own qualifications and seek better employment.

Tadeusz Brzeziński, in an agreement with the authorities of a technical college in Montreal, arranged for Polish professors and technical professionals to establish the first department of aeronautics at the college. Its first lecturers included professors Mokrzycki, Szczeniowski, Grzedzielski and Pawlikowski.

In his capacity as the representative of the Polish Government in Exile, Tadeusz Brzeziński held talks with Czechs and Slovaks, and with Consul General Pavlasek, concerning a possible federation of Poland and Czechoslovakia after the victorious war. This project had wide popular support. Meetings were held in Montreal and Toronto. Those taking part included Minister Jan Masaryk and Senator Vojta Beneš for the Czechs, and Brzeziński and

Professor Oskar Halecki for the Poles. However, when Germany attacked the Soviet Union in 1941 and the latter country found itself in the Allied camp, the Czechs shifted their support to the Soviets and the project collapsed.

Tadeusz Brzeziński remained faithful to the idea of a Polish-Czech accord, and felt the federation could have increased the strength and efforts of both nations.

In the meantime, several factors led to Polonia's deepening pessimism concerning the fate of the Polish nation: the discovery of the Katyn massacre; the tragic death of General Władysław Sikorski in July, 1943; the receipt of information concerning the threatened position of Poland's eastern territories; and the secret collusion at the Tehran Conference.

As usual in the face of danger, Canadian Poles made every effort to unite. The diplomacy and understanding of Tadeusz Brzeziński played a great part in the discussions that took place between the Polish Alliance, the Federation of Polish Associations and the Polish National Union.

In early September, 1944, as Warsaw staged an abortive uprising; the establishment of the Canadian Polish Congress was announced at a special convention in Toronto. The Congress was a federation of all the alliances, associations and parishes. Individual groups would continue to maintain their own aims, but all would present a united front for Polish causes, the good of Canada, Polish Canadians and their future.

This was a time of great warmth and sincerity on the part of Canadians toward the Polish cause. Quebec Premier Adelard Godbout issued a proclamation, "Homage a la Pologne," in which he praised Polish history and culture. By a decree of the Quebec legislature, a new county in the province's north was named Chopin. Lakes, rivers and mountains also received Polish names: Sobieski, Słowacki, Sienkiewicz, Mickiewicz, Kopernik, Paderewski, Piłsudski and Kosciuszko.

The political reality of postwar Poland was first voiced by Winston Churchill in a speech to the British House of Commons. Two months later Poland's situation and future were clearly delineated in the Treaty of Yalta.

In May, 1945, Tadeusz Brzeziński and General Sosnkowski travelled to western Canada to find places of settlement for demobilized Polish soldiers. They visited Winnipeg, Edmonton, Calgary and Vancouver. Brzeziński sent his report and suggestions to the Polish Government in Exile in London.

In July, 1945, Canada withdrew its recognition of the Polish Govenment in London. With that decision, Tadeusz Brzeziński was no longer Polish Consul General in Montreal.

In the autumn of 1946, the first transports of soldiers from the Polish Second Corps arrived from Italy—defeated by fate and political maneuvers. Soon after, demobilized soldiers from England began to arrive. According to Canadian immigration limits, the total number of these soldiers was not to exceed 4,500. The initial conditions which the newcomers faced were at best humiliating: two years of labour on farms at well below the minimum wage.

The majority of Poles, some several thousand, came to Canada under the internationally recognized "Displaced Persons"[4] program, which had been established for people from German concentration camps, other prisoners of war or members of the Home Army released from camps. At the same time, there arrived a transport of children who had survived exile to the Soviet Union and travelled to safety via India and Africa.

A total of 250,000 Poles arrived in Canada after the Second World War. Slowly, many of them migrated from the farms where they were first employed toward larger urban centers. Very few of the veterans chose to remain in farming after their experience of farm contract work. New organizations, made up of engineers, combatants, Home Army veterans, Nazi concentration camp survivors, airmen, etc., were formed.

Tadeusz Brzeziński later described this new wave of immigrants in the following way: "The newcomers, particularly the ex-army men, initially retained much of the spirit of 'Fighting Poland.' They stressed the temporary nature of their stay abroad. Besides the bitterness of their political memories, they betrayed a heavy dose of superiority in relation to their surroundings, setting themselves apart by their higher intellectual level and professional qualifications. This outlook did not lend itself toward assimilation—either into the older generation of Canadian Poles, or into the Anglo-Saxon society of their country of settlement, despite propitious relations and a generally friendly atmosphere. This outlook led also to the creation of their own organizations, not to the joining of already existing Polish groups; similarly, the soldiers viewed local surroundings as totally foreign, not their own . . . In time, however, several strong forces in various professions and in all walks of life made their marks in their new homelands."[5]

***

Tadeusz Brzeziński became the representative of the Polish-British Interim Treasury Committee, which had been formed in London to conclude business affairs and other matters started during the two nations' wartime cooperation. He was to fill this position until the end of January 1947.

On January 10, he received a letter from the Minister of External Affairs, Louis St. Laurent (later Prime Minister of Canada) reminding him of the upcoming end of his tenure. The letter read in part:

> With the disbanding of the Interim Treasury Committee, all the activities in Canada of the former Polish Government will have ceased. The Canadian Government does not recognize the existence of the former Polish Government in London which you, at one time, represented in this country. You may, however, continue to reside in Canada on the temporary permit which you now hold from the Director of Immigration. The permit will be subject to reconsid-

eration and renewal from year to year. During your stay in this country we would be grateful if you would refrain from any activities of a political nature which might suggest that you are remaining in Canada as representative of any official Polish organization.

Coming after eight years of continued cooperation, the letter was, as Brzeziński recalls, neither warm nor encouraging.

So Brzeziński began a new era in his life. First he had to find a job. "Official Canadian agencies," were no help at all. He found employment with Guardian Trust, a fifty-year old financial institution which had just opened a "department of Foreign Relations . . . to attend to correspondence in foreign countries and matters involving immigration." Tadeusz Brzeziński became head of the new department. Over the next three years, he was to help several hundred Poles immigrate and find jobs in their new country.

The Brzeziński family began a new phase in their lives: it was a time of "settling down."

Leonia Brzeziński was an extraordinarily active companion to her husband. A graduate of the Political Science School and the Music Conservatory in Warsaw, she spent the years in northern France, Leipzig and Saxony doing philanthropic work, aiding the poor and infirm. After the outbreak of the war in 1939, she headed the Polish section of the Canadian Red Cross in Montreal, raising money and supplies for Poland.

After the war, Leonia with her son Adam's assistance, opened a cosmetics laboratory in Montreal, and began selling her line of cosmetics under the name "Lady Beauty Products." The local press gave the firm much coverage, printing articles such as "Montreal Woman Makes Her Own Cosmetics 'Lady Beauty Products'," and "Polish Recipes for Skin Care Made Here for Canadian Women."

The Brzezinski's purchased a farm fifty miles outside of Montreal, in the Laurentians. They called it the "White and Red Farm." In summer, visitors would swim in the nearby Simone River; in fall, friends and neighbouring farmers would join the Brzezinski's for mushroom-picking; and in winter, for skiing. The farm became a frequently visited site for Polish Canadians. For some, it was the closest they could imagine to the Lower Carpathians back in Poland.

For over thirty years, this idyllic spot would be the recreational haven for the Brzeziński family.

On Tadeusz Brzezinski's initiative, the Roman Catholic priest in St. Saveur, the community just a few miles from the farm, agreed to designate part of the local cemetery for Poles. A number of distinguished Polish diplomats and war veterans are buried there: Babiński, Romer, Adamkiewicz, Gruszka, and General Szylling. A memorial to Adam Brzeziński, who died young, can also be found there.

Tadeusz Brzeziński became a Canadian citizen in May, 1951. He felt it his duty to become a citizen of the country which had given him and so many other Poles refuge. "I would never have repaid my debt to Canada if I had remained outside her society," he maintains. "And, being a Canadian, I found I could do more for Poland."

Both the Polonia and Canadian media reported on Brzeziński's decision to become a citizen. Over the next few years statistics would reveal a growing number of Poles taking out Canadian citizenship. During the early 1940's, only 33% of the Polish community were Canadian citizens. That figure more than doubled over the next ten to fifteen years.

One of Tadeusz Brzeziński's personal friends from the war years was George Drew, Premier of Ontario, and later federal leader of the Progressive Conservative Party in Canada. Drew suggested to Brzeziński that he run for parliament for the Conservatives in the Montreal riding of Cartier. Brzeziński accepted, though he knew his chances were minimal: the Cartier riding traditionally voted Liberal. Brzeziński himself was more a Liberal than a Conservative, yet he felt the candidacy of a Canadian Pole would ensure Polonia a voice, and would destroy the belief that public life—a political career—was reserved only for Canadians of English or French background.

He wrote:

> The atavism of a colonial country is unfortunately impeding the development of Canada, this land of promise . . . British and French citizens who call themselves 'founding fathers' have not, over the one-hundred year history of this nation, created any kind of common Canadian solidarity or patriotism, nor any vision of development and growth. They did not have their own constitution. Its surrogate is the British North America Act of 1867 (Forty Years with Canadian Poles: Memoirs).

The number of Poles who could help Brzeziński by voting for him was indeed small.

On July 18, 1953, the "Montreal Gazette" wrote:

> The nomination of Tadeusz Brzeziński is a choice that should be hailed by all Canadians, regardless of party. Not only is the former Polish diplomat, now a Canadian citizen, eminently well qualified to represent the multilingual electorate of this cosmopolitan constituency; he can bring to the foreign policy debate of the Commons a knowledge of East European politics that is almost unique.

Brzeziński lost the election of August 10, 1954. Nonetheless, he was one of the first Canadians of Polish descent in Montreal to run for the House of Commons. During the next election, in 1957, a Canadian Pole, Dr. Stanley Haidasz, was elected to represent the Toronto riding of Trinity. Up till then, the only parliamentarians of Polish descent had been Aleksander Edward Kierzkowski, elected provincially in 1830, and Maksymilian Globenski, a Conservative, elected to parliament from the country of Deux Montagnes in 1875.

In February, 1952, Tadeusz Brzeziński became President of The Canadian Polish Congress. He began implementing the Congress' tasks through the formulation of the following principles:

1. The Congress represents Canadians of Polish descent and expresses their collective will before federal and provincial authorities, before ethnic and religious groups, before the press and public opinion;
2. With respect to Canada, the Congress advocates full civil loyalty and active participation of Canadian Poles in Canadian life, while maintaining Polish national traditions and culture, as well as spiritual ties with the Polish Nation;
3. The Congress endorses the idea of Canadian unity by simultaneously recognizing the aspirations of French Canadians, and according a special place for the province of Quebec;
4. The Congress supports the right of the Polish Nation to full and autonomous sovereignty and civil liberty; at the same time the Congress retains its own independence from political influence in Poland and abroad.

Brzeziński was extremely active during his ten years tenure as President of the Canadian Polish Congress. He introduced a number of anniversary celebrations: on May 3 and November 11, parades complete with flags, marching bands and standards were held in Montreal. Several hundred people took part in these events. The city rang with music. The young people wore folk costumes modeled on characters from bygone eras, which were designed by noted costumist Tadeusz Slesicki. The local press eagerly covered the events, and these Polish parades even entered the tourist brochures as permanent attractions of the city of Montreal. People would gather for early Mass at the Cathedral, and then the parade would begin. Very often a government representative was invited to open the proceedings.

A Polonia delegation always took part in the French Canadian celebration of St. Jean Baptiste Day. The Canadian Polish Congress was represented by a team of horseback riders bearing standards.

Brzeziński initiated the annual Polonia New Year's Eve Ball. Often over 1,000 people attended the ball, which was held in the National Assembly. The mayor of the city of Montreal was invited, and the dancing always began with the traditional "Polonaise."

Unfortunately, all these gala celebrations slowly died out after Brzeziński's tenure. It's a pity, because they were a fascinating, effective way of presenting the Polish community to their fellow Canadians. In Canada as in the U. S., local parades are a way of life. These parades, which are far more popular on this continent than in Europe, enjoy a special significance and historical place in North American culture.

As Congress President, Brzeziński travelled to all the large Polonia centers across Canada. He maintained close contact with all the different organizations; attended meetings; and took part in campaigns and other celebrations. He was aware that through his participation he both supported and honoured the continuity and common good of the Polish community in Canada.

Under Tadeusz Brzeziński's guidance, an annual demonstration was held every September 1, with the motto: "Justice for Poland." The demonstration served to remind the community at large of the Poles' participation in World War II, and the war's subsequent political effects on Poland.

In 1956, a delegation of the Canadian Polish Congress met with Prime Minister Louis St. Laurent to discuss matters of importance to the Polonia community. The Polish presence in Canada was growing stronger and beginning to feel confident of its role and significance in public and political life. One of the delegation's requests was for the appointment of a Canadian Pole to the Senate. The delegation was made up of Dr. Brzeziński, Dr. Stanley Haidasz, Colonel Stefan Sznuk (former Minister Plenipotentiary of the Polish Government), lawyer Jan Ostrowski (president of the Toronto district of the Canadian Polish Congress), Jan Kurosad and Franciszek Głogowski, editor of "Związkowiec" (The Alliancer newspaper). The government agreed to take the Poles' suggestion into consideration. Candidates for a Senate appointment were Dr. Brzeziński, Colonel Sznuk and Bernard Dubienski, a lawyer and Polonia activist.

It was another twenty years before the Polish community was honored by the nomination of a senator from its midst. In 1978, Dr. Stanley Haidasz, one of the delegates from that very first visit, became a member of the Canadian Senate.

In January and May of 1956, Brzeziński published a series of articles in the Paris monthly "Kultura" (Culture), suggesting the activation of Poles abroad through the cooperation of central Polonia organizations and the formation of a World Council of Communication or a World Congress of Poles Abroad.

On May 3, an appeal signed by Congress President Jan Kurosad and General Secretary Antoni Malatynski was made to the central Polonia organizations around the world. The appeal proposed regional discussions on the formation of a World Polonia Congress, and an eventual world conference of Poles living abroad.

The appeal stated in part:

1. We are Poles living abroad. We have settled on different continents. We have become citizens of a number of different countries. In loyal cooperation with our fellow citizens, we are building a new life in other societies. Yet we are joined in the awareness of our Polish heritage, our attachment to Polish culture and national traditions, as well as our faith in the ideals of freedom and democracy;"
2. By this Act, we recognize the propriety of establishing a world organization of Polish communities abroad;"
3. The common organization is to be characterized by ideological cooperation, while retaining the absolute independence of regional organizations;"
4. The organization should be directed by democratic principles in its ideological premises, in its election of officers and organs, and in its internal administration."
5. The purpose of the organization is:

    a. To demonstrate the existence of the multi-million strong multitude of Poles living abroad, their united and independent front;

    b. To create and maintain solidarity before the most important Polish issues of today."

The appeal became the start of a long, animated debate that was aired in Polish media around the world. The most positive reaction came from the Polish communities in Canada, Australia and Argentina. American Polonia, with President Karol Rozmarek at its head, reacted very skeptically to the proposal, just as it had during the formation of "Swiatpol" in Warsaw in the 1930's. British Polonia, led by Adam Ciołkosz, also adopted a similarly negative attitude . . . The proposed convention of the World Congress of Polonia Abroad, which was slated for 1966 to coincide with the 1000th anniversary of the Polish Nation, never materialized.

In 1957, Brzeziński made a second appeal to organize Poles living abroad. In an article in "Związkowiec" on October 26, 1957, entitled "Changes in Poland and Poles Abroad," he wrote:

> This notion becomes all the more imperative in the present situation when, on the one hand, the 'immigrant state,' having fulfilled its mission, is passing into history before our very eyes; on the other hand, back in Poland the contours of the nation are once again emerging from the depths of oppression.
>
> One expression of Polonia's understanding of this situation is the proposal of the Canadian Polish Congress, initiated a year ago, suggesting a consideration of the possibilities of convening representatives of all Polish centers in the free world to collectively decide on the overall issue and purpose of establishing a common representation of Poles living abroad.

This initiative aims to logically complement the already existing regional Polonia organizations, by combining their strengths, with the support of all Poles living abroad, with a sound democratic base and financial independence. Long-term planning and designs for such a permanent organization of Poles abroad seem to lie in our national interest. The establishment of such an organ would strengthen the conviction in the homeland that Poles abroad are a positive entity on which the nation as a whole can depend.

Twelve years after the initial appeal—in 1978—the World Conference of Poles Abroad took place in Toronto. Brzeziński's vision came true. He did not, however, take part in the conference himself.

In 1954, on a recommendation from, among others, the Deputy Premier of Quebec, Tadeusz Brzeziński was hired by the Public Library in Montreal to work on research on Eastern Europe. Several years later the newly-established Ministry of Culture in Quebec formed a separate department in the Public Library in Montreal, called "Cultural Exhibits." The Library's Director, Georges Cartier, named Tadeusz Brzeziński head of the new department. Brzeziński remained in this position until his retirement in 1967. When he did retire he received the following special letter of gratitude from Mr. Cartier:

Dear Mr. Brzeziński,

Although since your official departure last February I have had the occasion to thank you publicly for the distinguished cooperation which you contributed during the several years we were able to work together at the St. Sulpice Library, and although I was able once again to express my appreciation when you definitively left our institution in April, I have intended to write you, since that time, to thank you for the excellent work you did, with such diplomacy and determination as I have never previously encountered.

In a few short months you were able to endow the St. Sulpice Library with a service of cultural exhibits and you established with such ease a full programme of seasonal activities, which have brought the Library a reputation which no other service could ensure it on such a large scale.

I would like now to express my sincere gratitude to you and to assure you my fondest and most loyal memory. I hope the future will grant you many more ample opportunities to channel the remarkable energy with which you have always proven yourself.

Georges Cartier Curator

The work brought Brzeziński much satisfaction, as well as recognition from others. He organized lectures, concerts, theatre and ballet productions, evenings devoted to different cultures, film screenings, art exhibits, and book and memorabilia displays.

The Canadian Polish Congress itself took advantage of the hospitality of the Public Library in Montreal, using library facilities for some of its Polonia functions.

After his official retirement, Brzeziński continued to work for the Public Library for two more years. In addition, he coordinated the activities of several cultural centers throughout Quebec under the auspices of the newly formed Federation of Cultural Centers of Quebec.

He participated actively in the work of the Polish Institute of Arts and Sciences in Montreal, which he had helped found in 1943. He was Vice-President of the Institute for several years, during which time he organized cultural events and lecture evenings, and also presented his own papers on politics, law and Polonia life.

After October 1956, the Polish community in Canada and throughout the world resumed efforts to establish contact with and provide assistance for fellow Poles in the homeland.

Brzeziński called a meeting of the Congress Executive Council in Toronto on November 24, 1956. The Council decided to institute a collection campaign using the slogan "Bread for Poland." They managed to collect $200,000 in just a few months. After negotiations, and with the help of Stefan Cardinal Wyszyński in Poland, the Central Executive Committee of the Aid for Poland Fund in Toronto undertook to distribute the money. Most of the collection was used for medical and hospital supplies, for example, for the purchase of a cobalt bomb and a dialysis machine. Other funds went to the Catholic University of Lublin, as well as to needy individuals.

Permanent lines of communication were established with Poland. The liner "Batory" began regular voyages between the two countries. There were more and more charters from Poland to Canada on "LOT" Polish airlines. (In 1971, "LOT" opened an office in Montreal; in 1976, permanent scheduled flights were established between Warsaw and Montreal.)

In 1959, Tadeusz Brzeziński returned to Poland for the first time in twenty-one years. He later sketched his impression for the Canadian Polish press:

"The first dazzling reaction upon reaching Warsaw is the confirmation of one's ties to the homeland . . . It gives one an invigorating awareness that—despite various turns of fate—we had not drifted too far apart and there is no great abyss between us, despite the passage of time, distance and changing conditions of existence . . . Credit for this goes above all to the people. A people of deep traditions, talented and patriotic, tied emotionally to the freedom and culture of the West, intelligent, experienced in misfortune, will not permit them to be shackled uncritically, passively. By their own strength they have, thus far, managed to resist attempts at shaping them into a new model . . . After only a brief observation, one quickly realizes that the Polish nation, that is to say at least 95% of the population, live their own lives, totally removed from the life of the governing few."[6]

"A few months ago I visited Poland for the first time in twenty-one years. I do not, of course, endorse the political state imposed on the nation. Nonetheless, I returned with a feeling of profound admiration for the people who, in such exceedingly difficult conditions, still strive for a better future. I was especially moved by the young people, a generation reared amid ruins and commentaries, yet still full of life, energy and beauty."[7]

In October 1959, a series of articles appeared in the Canadian Polish press accusing Brzeziński of . . . collaboration with the Polish authorities. Under the large, provocative headline, "With Whom Does One Drink Coffee?", Artur Tarnowski, President of the Union of Poles, criticized Brzeziński for having associated with a representative of the communist regime, and demanded that Brzeziński resign the presidency of the Montreal district of the Congress. The whole affair died eventually, but in retrospect the incident demonstrates the fact that almost every public figure in Polonia had, at one time or another, been accused or criticized for contact or even collaboration with the regime. Brzeziński wonders if this wasn't a kind of baptism that every aspiring Pole had to endure from his fellow immigrants.

The return to Poland of the Wawel Castle treasures and Chopin manuscripts is a truly fascinating tale. Tadeusz Brzeziński played an important role in these negotiations as well. While still Polish consul at Leipzig in the 1930's, Brzeziński discovered a collection of fifty Chopin manuscripts in the basement of a local publishing house, Breitkopf and Haertel. He urged the Polish government to purchase the documents.

The Wawel Castle treasures consisted of 136 Arrases, the "Szczerbiec" royal coronation sword (used as early as the XIV century), royal insignia, incunabula, medieval manuscripts, first editions of the Psalter and Bible, the oldest chronicles, as well as standards and armour.

The Chopin manuscripts and Wawel Castle treasures were smuggled out of Poland in September, 1939. They travelled through Rumania, France and England to Canada, where they were stored on an experimental farm outside Ottawa. During the war, under an agreement with the Polish Government in Exile, the treasures were insured. Therefore, in March 1945, the Chopin manuscripts, the chronicles, the Psalter, the coronation sword and the royal insignia were transferred to a vault in the Bank of Montreal in Ottawa. The remainder of the treasures, the Arrases, armours and royal standards, were placed in a convent outside Quebec City.

The Arrases were looked after by two curators, Jozef Polkowski and Dr. Swierz Zaleski. Ottawa envoy Dr. Wacław Babiński supervised the treasures for the Polish Government in Exile.

In May 1946, Dr. Albert Fiderkiewicz, a member of parliament from the Polish People's Republic, visited Canada. During a press interview, he complained that the Wawel Castle treasures were being hidden "by Catholic circles in Quebec." The exiled Government in London reacted quickly, and asked that the Arrases and other items be moved. Late at night, and in great stealth, envoy Babiński and curator Polkowski had the treasures moved to a cloister in Quebec City (Swierz Zaleski had in the mean time returned to Poland). The Canadian press began covering the story, publishing several articles and photographs of the hidden treasures. Albert Fiderkiewicz appealed officially to the government of Canada for the return of the valuables to Poland. The Mounted Police took up the case, but were anticipated by the local Quebec police force, which moved the treasures to the provincial museum in Quebec. There they were placed, free of charge, in a specially sealed vault designed for priceless collections.

Several years passed. After October 1956, various people—both in Poland and abroad—appealed for the return of the national treasures. In Poland, the Primate, Cardinal Wyszyński, and various religious, academic and cultural leaders all requested that the treasures be returned for the sake of the education of future generations, and for the good of all Poles. Individual artists and scholars joined in the appeal. Witold Malcuzynski, who held a concert tour in Poland in May, 1958, returned to Canada with a collective request from Polish musicians for the return of the Chopin manuscripts.

In October 1958, a special session of the Canadian Polish Congress was convened. In a separate resolution, Congress members sought immediate action to place the treasures under museum care. Congress moved that one possibility for such care would be the return of the collection to Poland, where professional curators could safeguard the treasures properly.

On October 14, 1958, Tadeusz Brzeziński personally gave the Congress resolution to Witold Malcuzynski, who in turn relayed it to Poland. Soon after, a delegation from Poland arrived in Canada and in early February, 1959, the first part of the treasures—the Ottawa collection—was shipped to Warsaw.

The Arrases and other items remained in the underground vault of the provincial museum in Quebec. Negotiations, appeals and requests for the return of these treasures continued for two more years. Public opinion both in Poland and among immigrants favored the return of the national treasures to Poland. One important voice raised in support of this position belonged to Bishop J. C. Cody of London, Ontario, who had recently returned from a pilgrimage to Częstochowa and was deeply impressed by the religiousness of the Polish people. Bishop Cody strongly urged that the treasures be sent back to Poland. When the Premier of Quebec, Maurice Duplessis—who opposed the return of the treasures—died, his successor, Paul Sauve and Antonio Barrette, began negotiations for their return.

Tadeusz Brzeziński voiced his opinion in the Canadian press—English, French and Polish—saying the valuables should be returned " . . . for the good of the nation and future generations." He also spoke on radio and at Canadian Polish Congress meetings. He was opposed by the representative of the Polish Government in Exile, Oktawian Jastrzembski, whose views, however, did not enjoy public support.

Ultimately, in Noveihber 1959, the Executive council of the Canadian Polish Congress passed a motion in support of the return of the treasures to Poland. The next premier of Quebec, Jean Lesage, made the final decision. Accordingly, in January 1961, the remainder of the Wawel Castle treasures, including the Arrases, made their way back to Poland in time for the 1000th anniversary of the Polish Nation.

Writing of the affair in his memoirs, Tadeusz Brzeziński noted:

"It is important and worthy of note that the entire affair was resolved successfully not through the compromises of official parties involved. The understanding was reached through communication between the homeland and the Polish community abroad, beyond governments, in the interest of the people, for their own good and the good of future generations."

Early in 1960, Tadeusz Brzeziński published an article entitled: "Polonia and the Millenium" which was carried by immigrant papers throughout the world. In the article, Brzeziński proposed the establishment of a National Culture Fund in all large Polish centers abroad. In Toronto the Committee for the 1000th Anniversary Celebrations was set up, and in turn established the Millenium Fund. In Montreal, the Maria Skłodowska-Curie Home for the Aged was opened.

In 1962, after ten years with the Canadian Polish Congress, Tadeusz Brzeziński resigned all his official duties. A banquet was held in his honor on March 4, 1962, at the hall of the Society for Mutual Aid. The new Congress President, Dr. Zbigniew Jurczynski, thanked his predecessor for his work, adding that the ten years period of his tenure would be remembered as "The Age of Brzeziński." In surveying those years and all the campaigns—both Polish and Canadian Polish—and their significance and value, and the tempered, diplomatic way in which they were executed, one can see the truth in Jurczynski's description: that decade was indeed "The Age of Brzeziński."

Tadeusz Brzeziński did not entirely withdraw from later Polonia activities and plans. Every once in a while an article of his would appear in the Canadian Polish press concerning Canadian, Polonia, or purely Polish matters.

In 1971 he devoted an article to the province of Quebec. The world's attention was focused on Quebec when Pime Minister Trudeau invoked martial law in the province on September 16, 1971. Brzeziński wrote that Quebec was not just another province like all the others; it was the only province with its own specific history, language, and traditions, and its own national identity based on its territory and population.

Eight years previously, in 1963, Brzeziński had commented on Prime Minister Lester Pearson's newly formed Royal Commission on Bilingualism and Biculturalism: "The very name of the Commission is in a way ambiguous and erroneous—it appears to take into consideration only two cultures in this country, and appears to prejudge that only two cultures can conclusively make up the whole of Canadian culture...

In fact, Canada's cultural foundation is made up today not of two cultures, but of several different national cultures—and the whole of Canadian culture, which we see developing before our very eyes, will not be merely British and French stripes, nor a checked pattern of ethnic influences. Rather, it should be the happy product of the combination of all these national cultures, starting with English and French, which together make up Canada's population."[8]

In October, 1971, Prime Minister Trudeau announced his multiculturalism policy, confirming that Canada was made up of more than two cultures. Writing on this subject some twelve years earlier, Brzeziński had stated:

> The principle of 'Canadianism' implies that each ethnic group should contribute the maximum of its values to the common spiritual nature of our future Canada. And it follows that the more valuable the contribution, the greater the advantage in the future.
>
> A person with no parents is an orphan. Similarly, a person with no spiritual heritage is an orphan in the spiritual sense. A Polish Canadian, without contributing his own inherited traditions, would also be an orphan, handicapped in comparison with other ethnic groups.
>
> Adopting a foreign cultural heritage will not help in this case. A Polish Canadian will not enrich Canada through English traditions, even if he knows all of Shakespeare by heart. Canada will expect his contribution to come from Polish culture. Assimilation or discrimination will serve only to impoverish Canada. There may be an official language, but not an official culture. Therefore, all ethnic groups can and should participate in the creation of a Canadian culture, thereby contributing to the sense of unity in the nation.

In January 1972, Brzeziński made an appeal to the Canadian Polish community for contributions toward the reconstruction of the Royal Castle in Warsaw, which had been bombed during the Second World War. In July of the same year, Professor Stanisław Lorentz, a man dedicated to Polish culture, visited Canada. Professor Lorentz, who was particularly interested in the restoration of historical monuments, also asked Polonia for assistance in the reconstruction of the Castle. Brzeziński gave his full support to the campaign, attending a special meeting organized by the President of the Polish Alliance in Canada, Tadeusz Glista, at Place Polonaise in Grimsby, Ontario. The drive was also endorsed by then Executive President of the Canadian Polish Congress, Kazimierz Bielski.

Brzeziński wrote: "The Royal Castle in Warsaw is an important symbol. It represents the royal majesty of the Republic, underlining the continuity of Polish statehood. It is irrefutably a part of the character and panorama of the capital city. Since the XVII century it has been the seat of Polish kings, and the scene of many historical events. The Constitution of the 3rd of May was ratified in its Senate Chamber. To destroy the castle was to strike the nation at its heart; such was the criminal intent of the occupying German forces. To rebuild the castle is to return to the Polish capital its hallmark of tradition and splendour."[9]

On the same occasion, Brzeziński chose to speak out on the plans to have King Stanisław August's remains returned to Poland:

> The reconstruction of the castle brings to mind one more matter of 'unfinished business.' To this day, the remains of Poland's last king have not returned to Warsaw . . . It can be said that Stanisław August Poniatowski was the most Warsovian of Polish kings. Warsaw has Stanisław August to thank for the fact that, following the darkness of the Saxon reign, the capital became the centre of the Polish Enlightenment. During Stanisław August's reign, Warsaw saw the creation of the first Ministry of National Education in the world, the first public theatre in Poland, the first military academy, known as the School of Knights. On his initiative, the Łazienki Palace was built. Stanisław August gave special attention to the development of education, literature and art. Many writers and artists thrived under his inspiration and protection. Failures in the political realm found their consolation in the progress of culture, which had its life-center in the king and castle . . . As the new royal castle rises on the Warsaw horizon, one must not forget the man who left it standing for the Polish Nation: Stanisław August died is St. Petersburg after the last partition of Poland. He was buried in the crypt of the Church of St. Catharine. One hundred and forty years later the coffin was returned to Poland shortly before the outbreak of the Second World War. It was placed temporarily in Wolszyn, near Brest, where Stanisław August was born. Should it not make its last journey to Warsaw, to its final resting place in the walls of the Stanisław Chapel of the Royal Castle? The fact that Wolszyn, since the end of the war, is outside Poland should not be a hindrance. The reconstruction of the castle brings this matter to the fore once again—a matter which lies heavily on the heart of many Poles and has already been the subject of much discussion. [10]

Tadeusz Brzeziński carried on a long correspondence with Pofessor Lorentz concerning the reconstruction of the castle and the return of the remains of Stanisław August. One of Professor Lorentz's letters was published in "Związkowiec" on April 11, 1972:

> I am in complete agreement that the remains of King Stanisław August should be returned to Warsaw. Because the chapel in the castle is rather small and not all in the manner of a mausoleum, I propose that one wing of the main palace in the Łazienki Park be transformed into the mausoleum of Stanisław August Poniatowski. The figure of the king has recently been presented in a new light by historians, and his contributions to Poland have been assessed very highly. A work by Dr. Emanuel Rostworowski entitled "The Last King of the Respublica" and a recently published book by Paweł Jasienica confirm this development.

I think we will meet our deadline and the castle exterior will be completed by the summer of 1974. We will then begin work on the historic interior. Efforts are continuing to return the remains of Stanisław August. I think they will soon end successfully.

Many articles and new assessments of Poland's last king have been published. (A particularly fascinating work by Marian Brandys appears in the Paris journal "Kultura" under the title "My Adventures with History: The Sentry at the Royal Tomb.") Nonetheless, Stanisław August's coffin still remains outside Poland. Professor Lorentz, one of the most active fighters in this cause, died in 1982. Who will now take up the fight?

***

Tadeusz Brzeziński was chairman of a committee which organized a congress of academics and writers of Polish origin in May 1975 at McGill University in Montreal. More than four hundred participants arrived from America, Europe, Australia and Asia. Over 185 papers were presented by 18 panels. Based on his experiences at the congress, Brzeziński sent a questionnaire to academics and writers of Polish origin living abroad, seeking their opinion on Polish world intellectual cooperation. He wrote:

> The cultural avant-garde of the Polish Diaspora should not disappear with the passage of time. It is in the nation's interest to ensure it possibilities for further development and closer ties. Natural tendencies in this direction have already demonstrated themselves in various conferences and congresses, in the establishment of Polish research institutes, cultural foundations, libraries, museums, in the initiation of contests, questionnaires, in commonly sponsored events in various places for various occasions. [11]

Tadeusz Brzeziński remains closely associated with the Polish Institute of Arts and Sciences in Montreal and the Canadian Polish Research Institute in Toronto (founded in 1956). Brzezinski's paper entitled "Canadian Poles Yesterday and Today," presented in January 1974, was published in English in Volume VIII of the Canadian Polish Research Institute's publications, under the title: Past and Present.

In 1972, Brzeziński was jury chairman for a competition for memoirs by Polish immigrants. Fifty-two entries were submitted. A selection of these memoirs, which were edited by Benedykt Heydenkorn, appeared in three volumes entitled "Memoirs of Polish Immigrants."

Brzeziński has donated all his papers and archival materials to the National Archives in Ottawa, where they form "The Tadeusz Brzeziński Collection."

In 1976, on the occasion of Tadeusz Brzeziński's eightieth birthday, a number of articles were written in his honor. The Executive President of the Canadian Polish Congress, Władysław Gertler, wrote: "You have contributed so much good, so many positive acts to Canadian Polish life over the years that the community will be ever indebted to you."

I first met Tadeusz Brzeziński on a sunny October day in 1982 at the Polish Institute of Arts and Sciences in Montreal. He is an elegant and charming man. He asked me what I thought of Montreal. Then he gave his own impressions not only of Montreal, but also of some of the other cities of the world he knows so well.

> I like Montreal, the city has a lot of joie de vivre. Mount Royal gives it much added charm. Toronto is a business town . . . What city do I remember most fondly? Vienna. A very pleasant place in which to live. It doesn't have the heaviness of so many German cities. Paris also has all of Vienna's charms, plus a greater freedom which, in certain, more puritanical times, I found very attractive. I also think Warsaw is an extraordinary warm city. I wouldn't like to live in New York. It's too violent . . .

I asked him about his principles and what had guided him in his relations with others. Even after so many years, his recounting of events, his meetings with people, his tales were all warmly told; his judgments were tempered and rational. He did not convey—as sometimes happens—any harbored dislikes or negative emotions toward others. When I pressed him on this, he replied:

> Courtesy and truth always assisted me both in the world and in Canadian Polish life. I was born 'polite' and quite urbane . . . You want to add 'elegant'? In Przemyśl, my father used to be called *arbiter alegantiorum* . . . As far as my relations with people are concerned . . . You know, when one has to deal with a great number of people, almost all over the world, one gains experience, insight. I also have the abilities and experience of a diplomat, though I don't want to exaggerate this diplomacy, it could lead to the absurd.
>
> If I don't like someone, I try to avoid him, that way I minimize my chances of becoming irritated. I can always find something to discuss with another person, a topic he or she likes, and is very familiar with . . .
>
> I'm optimistic by nature. That has always helped me in life.
>
> With age a person becomes less argumentative, more understanding and intelligent. He tends to avoid conflicts. That's how it is in my case.
>
> . . . What else would I like to accomplish? There are a number of things. One of them . . . is the successful completion of the campaign I began with Professor Lorentz; that is, the return to Poland of the remains of Stanisław August, and also Chopin's coffin. As a great enthusiast of Chopin's music (I play the piano myself, though I'm not greatly talented), I feel his remains should also be in Poland. In the Pere La Chaise cemetery in Paris, there is just a modest head stone marking the composer's grave, and not many people are interested in it. In Poland Chopin's grave would be visited often. A number of problems have arisen in connection with these campaigns, most of them stemming from Warsaw. I had a friend in Paris, the son of a participant in the January (1863) Uprising. His name was Jean Paul Palewski. He was interested

in having Chopin's coffin returned to Poland. Unfortunately, both he and Professor Lorentz have passed away. Who will look after these things now?

I visited Tadeusz Brzeziński again in May 1983, at his home on Monkland Avenue in Montreal. The rainy weather forced us to carry on our conversation inside. I was able to look at many of his photographs, documents, letters, and mementos. On the desk lay Zbigniew Brzeziński's latest book, Power and Principle: Memoirs of the National Security Adviser 1977-1981, with the dedication in Polish: Kochanym Rodzicom—Syn (To my Beloved Parents—from Their Son).

I asked him about many things and many people. Again I was struck by his humility, his unaffectedness and tact. Here was man who had been active in so many of this world's affairs, yet who could talk about them in a totally natural way.

Wherever he has lived—in Poland, Leipzig, Lille, Kharkov or Montreal—Tadeusz Brzeziński has always known how to give of himself, how to make permanent the fruit of his actions.

Such a large part of his life—over forty years—has been dedicated to Canadian Poles. For many years he was their leader, their symbol of authority. Above all, he has always been a man of action.

I wonder what Canadian Polish life would have been like without Dr. Tadeusz Brzeziński. Without his ideas, his appeals, his deeds. Certainly it would have been much poorer. And, by the same token, so too would have been the Polish cause, for which he has done so much.

Tadeusz Brzeziński died of pneumonia in Montreal at the age of 94, on January 7, 1991.

ZBIGNIEW BRZEZINSKI: POLAND-CANADA-USA

I talked to his son, Zbigniew Brzezinski and I asked about his childhood, Poland, Canada and USA.

Zbigniew came to Canada from Poland when you were ten years old. I asked about his memories of Poland. In his memoirs, Power and Principle, there is a beautiful passage in which he quotes from "Sophie's Choice" in which the author, William Styron, compares Poland to the southern United States. He answered:

> My recollections of Poland are manifold. I was a very patriotic child and I took enormous pride in the development of the country. I was very pleased to see Gdynia built up and was very proud that Poland had such a modern port. I was delighted to see the development of "Żoliborz" in Warsaw and "Saska Kepa," both good examples of modern development. I remember the countryside, the river San at Przemyśl, where I used to go bathing—my grandmother used to

live there. I particularly remember my scouting uniform, and the pride I took in winning badges. I especially recall the various annual military parades, especially those of May 3rd and November 11th. I was enormously proud of the Polish Army. I enjoyed watching it parade down the streets of Warsaw, and probably like many people of my generation, I had enormous confidence in its military capabilities.

A year after the Brzezinski family came to Canada, the war in Europe began. Tadeusz was actively interested in the Polish struggle. He (unsuccessfully) attempt to recruit volunteers for the Polish army in Windsor, Ontario.

Zbigniew told that he followed the war with passionate interest. They learned of the invasion early in the morning of September 1st 1939, and from then on they followed the events of the war on a daily basis. He read all the daily dispatches his father brought home from his office, notably those of PAT (Polska Agencja Telegraficzna). He visited the military barracks in Windsor as a guest of General Duch who was a Polish commander of the newly formed units in North America. As he looked back at the pages of the diary that he kept as a small boy, he is struck by the fact that he recorded not so much what he or his brothers or his parents were doing, but what happened or what happen in a given day during the war. His youthful diary is full of the events of the day and what was happening at the different fronts. He was especially fascinated by what was happening in Poland and followed with the greatest dedication and sense of personal involvement all the activities of the home army.

When the war ended, the political reality of post-war Poland caused Tadeusz Brzezinski to decide to stay permanently in Canada.

Zbigniew remembers vividly the end of the war. The students streamed out of the school, and marched down the main street of Montreal. Everyone was waving flags, mostly American, British and Russian. Curiously in that paroxysm of joy, he felt sad. He felt that Poland was again occupied. So while everyone was celebrating, he just went through the motions. He did not have feelings of joy. The war absorbed him so completely that he was emotionally and intellectually involved primarily in Poland's affairs. It was only after 1945 that he began to identify with Canada, and to appreciate its freedom, its enormous opportunity, the fundamental decency of its people and its system.

He became very much a part of Canada and I thought that Canada would be his second home. It was really a matter of chance that he ended up at Harvard, and saw the enormous opportunities that were opened up to him in the United States. He became more actively involved in American life. Moreover to the extent that he has always been interested in international affairs, he felt that he identified more and more with the United States. He felt that America had the greater capacity for influencing world affairs for the good, and thus helping to fashion a more just international system that would therefore also help Poland. Poland is the home of his childhood, the source of his historical and cultural identity, but Canada is the place where he first experienced mature consciousness, where he formed his first mature friendship's and had his first romantic experiences; it's the place where he really grew up.

His family lived in Montreal, a city with a very specific political and social reality. Zbigniew did not become too interested in Quebec until the late 1940-ies when his father started working for the province of Quebec, and increasingly identified with Quebecois aspirations. Only then did he fully appreciate the degree to which French Canadians really were second class citizens.

His contacts with the Canadian Polish people—"Polonia" were relatively limited and came primarily through his father. He admired the dedication and the determination of the first generation of Polish immigrants who struggled against adversity to shape for themselves a better life, and yet still retained their links with Poland. He particularly admired the group associated with the "Związkowiec" for they represented genuine dedication not only to Poland, but to truly democratic principles. Later on during WW II and afterwards, new waves of Poles, better educated than the first, came to Canada, and they also helped immensely to elevate the life of the Canadian "Polonia".

The most important aspect of growing up in Canada was his college experience. It was at McGill that he developed a definite political outlook and became interested in a systematic way, in Soviet studies. It was at McGill that he began to find a new purpose in life that was no longer focused so much on Poland, but saw him becoming increasingly involved in world affairs. Also his experience at McGill led to Harvard, which was clearly a very major take off stage to his subsequent life.

When he was doing his undergraduate work in Canada his intention was to enter the Canadian Foreign Service. When he graduated from McGill, he planned to study in the U. K., and had obtained a McGill fellowship to study there. He said—he doubtless would have come back from the U. K. to Canada and pursued a diplomatic career. However, at the last minute, it turned out that his not being a Canadian citizen meant that he could not take advantage of the McGill fellowship which he had won. As a result, he decided to study in the United States and went to Harvard. From then on his subsequent career, in a sense, took a new course largely dictated by the enormous opportunities that Harvard and America offered.

I asked about a problem: that Canada is very dependent on the United States both economically and culturally. He answered, that at the same time there are also certain advantages. If Canada was not located where it was, but was, let's say, isolated like New Zealand, it could be a much more parochial society than it is today. Canada is in fact a very cosmopolitan, outward oriented and increasingly sophisticated society, and this is at least in part due to its close interaction with the United States.

Asked if he had remained in Canada, does he think he would have followed a primarily academic career, or would have become involved in Canadian politics, he answered, that had he stayed in Canada he might have become a minister for External Affairs. However, there is no doubt that the process would have been more difficult than in the United States, which is more accustomed to "foreigners" rising to the top. Such a rise is a less probable phenomenon in Canada.

Zbigniew Brzezinski reached the highest political position accessible to someone who is not an American by birth. I remember the enthusiasm with which his appointment as President Carter's security advisor was greeted in Poland.

He answered that his career was, in part, the product of very deliberate determination. He wanted to be able to influence events, to meld thought with action. He considers this to be the highest human vocation. In this case, in so doing he wanted to accomplish something positive for America, for Poland, for the free world, and probably for people everywhere. But obviously you cannot achieve the things you set out to do in life unless fortune, good luck, and providence of a divine sort create the right moment, and the proper opportunity. He said he was lucky in that respect. He intends to pursue his vocation in the future, to combine thought and action in the hope that it serves some good.

He stressed the Polish traditions were very important to him; they helped shape him and they continue to influence his life, his instincts and his spontaneous reactions. It was, however, very difficult to transmit these traditions to children whose mother is not Polish and who does not use her own native tongue. His children (Ian, Mark and Mika) do not speak Polish. He has tried to make them proud of their Polish origin and to make them aware of the importance of Polish tradition and history.[12]

Zbigniew Brzezinski passed away at age of 89, on May 26, 2017.

NOTES

1. The part of this chapter appeared in 1984 in my book titled "Dreams and Reality. The Polish Canadians Identities" sponsored by the Ontario Ministry of Citizenship and Culture and the Adam Mickiewicz Foundation of Toronto. In Polish the book appeared under the title "Kanada, Kanada…", in Warsaw, 1986.

2. Tadeusz's father, Kazimierz (family crest: Trąby), was a judge in Przemysl. His grandfather, also Kazimierz, was the doctor of the Radziwill Family.

3. Tadeusz Brzezinski married Leonia Roman (1896-1985) (Leonia married first to Zylinski) who was a daughter of Leon Roman (family crest Ślepowron from the year 1612). The family estate was in Dąbinki near Radzymin. She was a granddaughter of Countess Leontyna Orłowska and Antoni Roman.

4. Displaced Person - an official connotation given by the United Nations Organization to refugees in Europe after WW II.
5. "Związkowiec", (The Alliancer), January 18 -19, 1974.
6. "Głos Polski", (Polish Voice), June 18, 1959.
7. "Związkowiec", (The Alliancer), September 9, 1959.
8. "Związkowiec", (The Alliancer), November 2, 1963.
9. "Związkowiec", (The Alliancer), January 18, 1972.
10. "Związkowiec", (The Alliancer), January 18, 1972.
11. "Kultura", Paris, May, 1911.
12. The oldest son of Zbigniew Brzezinski, Ian, is an American foreign policy and military affairs expert, having spent almost two years in Ukraine as a volunteer, helping the Ukrainians with their national security problems, then by working as the foreign policy advisor to Senator Roth, president of the North Atlantic Assembly. He served as Deputy Assistant Secretary of Defense for Europe and NATO Policy in 2001–2005, under President George W. Bush.

His second son, Mark, spent two years in Poland as a Fulbright scholar, both studying and occasionally teaching at the Warsaw University. He then went to Oxford, where he completed a doctorate, focusing on the introduction of constitutionalism into the Polish democracy. Mark Brzezinski was an American diplomat and was the United States Ambassador to Sweden from 2011 to 2015.

His daughter, Mika appears under her maiden name. She is a well known American television host, author and journalist. Brzezinski co-hosts MSNBC's weekday morning broadcast " Morning Joe" with former Republican representative Joe Scarborough. She is an author of "All Things at Once", "Knowing Your Value: Women, Money and Getting What You're Worth".

Zbigniew's younger brother, Lech Brzeziński, continues living in Montreal, where he is head of a large engineering company. His wife, Wanda (from Poland), has a medical practice. Their eldest child, Matthew, has become a newspaper reporter and has spent two years in Poland, then reporting from Kiev for the "Wall Street Journal".

Chapter Two

Two Great Passions —
Flying and Writing

Rudolf S. Falkowski

Although alone all his life, he wrote beautifully about love.

Two great passions pursued him; two great dreams possessed him.

As a young boy, then in the second grade of elementary school, he saw his first airplane—actually a biplane (an aircraft with two wings). He stared into the skies with awe and decided he would become a pilot. In Stanisławów[1], he began to fulfil his dream of flying by completing two glider courses during vacations from high school.

As an adult and by then a licensed pilot, he flew various types of British and American aircraft while serving in four English squadrons including the legendary Polish 303 squadron of Battle of Britain fame.

Falkowski's dream of becoming a writer never diminished.

Barely the age of ten, he started writing a personal journal, and his effort continued for another twenty years. Actually writing novels became part of a daily routine, as writing became his life-long passion. Writing for self satis-faction, he hoped deep inside that "some day someone would read it". Spend-ing long hours after work, each day found him at his desk bent over a sheet of paper.

At the age of 88, the pilot/author experienced the publication of his first book.

***

I first heard of Falkowski from Stefan Władysiuk, a librarian in the Polish Library in Montreal. Stefan sent me manuscript titled *Sprawa kapitana Am-reicha—The Case of Captain Amreich*, asking for my opinion of the author

Rudolf S. Falkowski's work. I knew nothing about him, only having general information that he was born in Czortków in Podolia[2] in April 1919.

The book turned out to be an interesting novel: suspenseful, captivating of interest, with nice, clear language.

A moving love story of Angelika and Borayski was presented, intricately woven with emotion, as well as side theme of the life of Amreich, a Jewish convert to Christianity. The events of the plot were set during World War II but extended also to the years before and after the war—years which were crucial, tragic and difficult ones in Polish history. The book presented one more human life conditioned by historic events. Reading it left you with nostalgic feelings, and mobilized you to ponder on the role of chance, human ambitions, yearnings, honor, promises, and expectations.

The novel was written in the third person, so that the Introduction written in the first person's voice seemed peculiar to me:

Many years have passed since that warm, starry August night of 1939, when for the last time I listened to my paramour, who was quietly singing along with Hanka Ordonówna[3], who in turn was singing on the Lviv radio: "Co nam zostało z tych lat miłości pierwszej . . . " [What do we have left from those years of first love . . .]

And now, sometimes, in quiet, starry nights, when I sit alone on the balcony of the fifteenth floor, when I look up into the stars, nostalgia puts a lump in my throat.

And I often think of Seneca, the Roman philosopher, and distinctly feel what he felt in his exile in Spain, speaking of "horas serenas"[4] . . .

Seneca can be found in each book on the history of philosophy, but I do not think we can find anywhere Hanka's songs, not anymore. I heard that during the war, in 1942-1943, she still sang in the USSR, in the newly forming Polish Army, and later in the Middle East.

But both Hanka and the Polish Army are long gone and forgotten. What remains is unquenchable nostalgia.

Author

The book *Sprawa kapitana Amreicha* was published in Montreal in 2009 by a private, sponsored publisher "Doliwa". It starts with Falkowski's portrait, painted in 1962 by Zofia Romer (wife to Tadeusz[5]). The author kindly sent me the book with an inscription:

To Dear Aleksandra with gratitude for the kind opinion on my talent
Sincerely yours
Rudolf Falkowski
Montreal, May 3, 2009

I became curious about Rudolf S. Falkowski, the author of the beautiful novel about love. In reply to my inquiry, Stefan Władysiuk sent me a 670-page volume titled *Żużle na dłoni—Cinder in My Hand*. I had been given Falkowski's first book, issued 2007 in Montreal.

Numerous pictures show a boy from Czortków in 1937, later pictures of a handsome young high school graduate from Stanisławów, subsequent pictures from the Pilot School in Stanisławów dated April 1939 and finally from the Kermine camp in Uzbekistan. Also, there are many pictures of him in a pilot's uniform in Scotland and in England, and some group pictures of the 303 Squadron.

This book—just like the typescript sent before—made a particular impression on me. The book, however, was not a novel but a compilation of notes made from 1929 until 1948. . . . not a diary, not reminiscences, but a journal with daily (!) entries.

Rudolf Falkowski started writing at the tender age of ten: he described various events, quoted conversations, made his own comments. Writing was clearly a pleasure for him, so he unfailingly filled subsequent notebooks. The journal holds much detail from his childhood spent in the south-eastern borderland[6] of Poland, depicting activities of early youth and school days in the gymnasium in Stanisławów.

The author shows a multicultural community, the feelings and mood concerning the oncoming war, and then its beginnings. He describes his attempts to escape to Hungary, mobilization and conscription into the Red Army, forced labor in Russia, successfully joining the 2nd Corps and flying with the RAF in the Polish 303 squadron. The journal also describes the end of the war and the author's decision to leave to Canada.

Falkowski wrote of a conflict with the professor who taught him Polish in the high school in Stanisławów. Criticising his Russianisms, the teacher said that "pigs are going to fly" the day that Rudolf writes something sensible in pure Polish. At that time, the boy was already writing his journal which now, on its publication, is a rich source for historians.

Continuing to be vengeful, the professor of Polish did not allow Falkowski to take the final exams, and thus, Rudolf started his military service by joining the Air Force Officer Training Centre a year later. In the summer of 1939, the aspiring pilot completed another course in pilotage, and in autumn, he planned to join the Pilot School in Stanisławów.

Meanwhile, historic events decided the course of his life, like they did with millions of others.

In May 1941, less than two months before Russia was attacked by Hitler, Falkowski was conscripted into the Red Army together with 200,000 young people of various nationalities, including Poles. The mobilization served as a major benefit to the Russians, as it minimized potential activities against them. The conscripted forces were not sent to the front but were directed to working battalions. Rudolf Falkowski, who spoke Ukrainian and Russian, was employed as a guard for trains carrying food and ammunition. He then worked in *sovkhozes*[7] and cleared forests cutting pines to be used in aircraft production. Subsequently, he graduated into the actual production of planes.

***

As a result of the Sikorski-Majski agreement of 30th July 1941, thanks to which the Polish Army was organized in the southern Soviet republics, Rudolf Falkowski was released from the Red Army in April 1942 and came to the pilots' camp in Kermine, Uzbekistan. From there, he and many others travelled by troop ship traversing the seas to Scotland.

The period from June 1942 until April 1948, he remembered as difficult years, but wonderful ones. The difficult years were due to his Red Army background that precipitated walls of prejudice towards him, but after a few months he was directed to further aviation training. After a year's course in advanced pilotage, he flew various types of aircraft—British fighters: Hurricanes, Spitfires, and American Mustangs, while serving in four British squadrons and the famous Polish 303 Squadron.[8]

After the war, Falkowski took a drafting course offered by the Polish Resettlement Corps in England, at the experimental station at Farnborough. Soon after completing the drafting course, he decided to immigrate to Canada.

He writes in the introduction:

> I brought my brief case with notes, newspaper clippings and pictures to Canada in April 1949.My accumulation of information on Canada had actually started in the autumn of 1929, due to a certain adventure near the Polish-Soviet border that I write about in the journal. At first, these were clumsy words written in great 'secrecy'. By the end of my formal schooling, a thick notebook had been filled with my notes. Then the war came, life under Soviet occupation was survived, hardships in Russia were endured in 1942, then my piloting career was fulfilled in England with the Polish 303 squadron. Jotting down everything about us—what could be seen, heard and read, until the arrival in Canada.

On the back cover, the following text is written:

> When he was ten, in 1929, together with his parents, he attended the wedding of his father's first cousin, who lived on the Zbrucz River at the Polish-Soviet border. During the feast, one of the guests, a Lieutenant of the Border Protection Corps[9] was given a 'tip': a bunch of smugglers and agitators were getting ready to cross the border from the Soviet side. At his father's request, the officer took the boy with him to his observation point.
> On return to their room, as he watched the officer making notes on the border incident in his journal, he decided to keep his own journal from that day on.

(. . .) The important thing is that it's been written down. The Russians say, "Shto napishesh perom, ne virubish toporom."[10] The Romans said, "Verba volant, scripta manent."[11] —Someone is going to read that.

Falkowski's journal starts with the note:

"1929, 2nd October, Friday, Czortków-Pastusze
We are going to a wedding in Nowosiółka Biskupia. Dad, Mom and myself. The groom is Piotr F, elderly bachelor, Father's first cousin.
At seven in the afternoon, we left from the Szmańkowczyki station. On the way, we passed small towns—Jezierzany, Teresin, Borszczów, Wołkowce-Turylce. We left the train at the Germakówka station. The next station was Iwanie-Puste, near Okopy Św.Trójcy[12], where the borders of the USSR, Romania and Poland meet.
The train slowly disappeared. The lights of the last car drew bright red threads chasing it down the tracks. They vanished at the curve. Everything looks different at night. That was my first trip by train.
Uncle was waiting for us with a cart. Two black horses gleamed in the large moon's glow. Midnight. We set off straight east down the broad road.
(. . .)

The note on the incident at the border opened his witnessing of twenty years of notes, descriptions, and observations.

As I was reading the journals, I found fragments, not many, which did not fit the rest, as they were written in contemporary times. They struck me as odd, since those were opinions the author could develop years later, e.g. when on 1st August 1945 he learned of the outbreak of the Warsaw Uprising. Those opinions included remarks about Stanisław Skalski, Miłosz, and Modzelewski[13]. A flashing of the names of Gomułka, Gierek and Jaruzelski[14]. Stefan Władysiuk confirmed my conjectures that when the journals were rewritten and adjusted by the author, he added some comments from looking back at those times. The author could have placed those modern remarks in an afterword, or a footnote. Still, those few fragments did not blur the strong impression of authenticity that resulted from reading the journals.

***

Having read *Żużle na dłoni*, I wrote a letter to Falkowski:

14th February 2009
Dear Rudolf,
From Stefan Władysiuk, I have received your book Żużle na dłoni.
I have been reading it for the last two weeks with unfailing interest. It contains scenes which remain in the reader's memory, and strikes with your nice language and great perceptiveness.

I found your description of the visit of General Sikorski and your remarks highly interesting.

Also, I was moved e.g. by the scene with the dog that wanted to jump on the train and go with the squadron . . . I must admit, I was somewhat surprised with your remark that you "realized 'in what sort of country you were living", as in general, you seem to have more sharp remarks against the British or even the Polish than against Russians.

All of that is highly interesting, and very authentic.

With best wishes
Aleksandra Ziółkowska-Boehm

I received a reply:

Montreal, 21/07/2009
My Dear Kind Lady,
Thank you so much for your last postcard. It reminded me of the time when I worked as a draftsman and tried drawing pictographs. Unfortunately, the previous physical work robbed my fingers of flexibility, but they worked well enough to hit the keys of a typewriter.

As concerns my book, it is like with a child born unto an old couple. Hard to say how and when it came about. It was rather planned to be an integral part of Żużle . . . . I gathered so much impetus in writing my journal that I slowed down only once after I had written a manuscript of a size of four times the volume of this tome. The one thing I knew was that no one would publish that, and I knew not what to do with it.

Stefan had a good answer to that, "You must make a thorough purge . . . No one will print a tome that size."—"Geez," I thought, "So much work," but I knew there was no other option. I understood that the only way was to give the journal a 'prudent' face. Gradually, I put away more personal, intimate pages, issues which were too controversial, facts which might have caused disbelief, and so on. That took nearly half the journal.

We went through the text with Stefan once again, and the book entered the world, to quote your words.

And thus what was left lay there for nearly half a year. Once, when I was planning to get rid of unnecessary, old papers, I felt like checking what I had actually put aside.

On reading a few pages I realized that in my hand I was holding enough material for another book. What struck me was that when writing the journal, there was no sentiment or tenderness, everything went matter of fact [sic], and now various controversies began to emerge, recollections, something like nostalgia, in particular when I was describing that last summer time in August 1939—as if I were watching "Gone with the Wind".

To be honest, that was the hardest time to write. There remained some unspecified regret that all of it ended like it did. But somehow I struggled through it, and resurrected everyone and everything I had not wanted to leave in the journal.

I learned that people do not believe facts much, but if the same fact is spiced up with some tasty fiction sauce, they would swallow it whole.

A few weeks ago, a friend of mine called me and said that on reading my book she was reminded of the film "Gone with the Wind". She wanted to know where I had learned to write books, because she had nothing to do and would like to write something, as well. I told her I had to live up to 90 to catch my wind. So she may try, she may even find it, but you never know with the wind.

But I would not wish to bore you. Currently I'm taking a peredishka, *a breather, and I'm reading books long forgotten. I found your* Dreams and Reality. *It brought back the good old times in Toronto—Mr Haidasz, editor of "Głos Polski", and also Żurakowski; him I knew back in England. His beloved test pilot flying finally tested him back. Pity.*

But I do feel I have bored you to death. Please excuse the familiarity of tone, but I can talk about such matters tête-à-tête *with no one here save for Stefan.*

And thus, Madam, in an old Lviv custom I wish all the good health on you as I kiss your hand and hope you take good care.

Rudolf Falkowski

We had long telephone conversations which brought answers to some of my questions. I asked Rudolf about his life in Canada.

At first, he was sent to Alberta, where he worked on a farm. Later in British Columbia, he cut pines, as he once did in Russia.

In the early 1950s, he settled in Toronto, where he worked among other forms of employment as a real estate agent and a door-to-door Bible salesman. At the same time, he took a few drafting courses over a four year period. On completing the courses, he found a position as an employee of the port of Montreal. Falkowski worked there continuously for 27 years—from December 1955 until his retirement in 1982. Montreal became his final place of residence.

Pen and paper remained his closest friends all his life. In Canada, he discontinued writing a journal, but wrote novels instead. He rewrote them several times, with corrections. He said that writing was a way of spending his leisure time, nearly an obsession. It was also a dream of many years that he would become a 'real writer'—i.e. that a book of his would be published. The notebooks containing his journal remained in his case for many years. When he retired, he read them anew.

Falkowski revealed to me that when young and at school, he had to be careful to hide his notebooks from classmates. The writing might be judged to be politically suspicious and thereby lead to the author's execution.

The author knew he had a need to write on a particular impulse. Writing during the war, and writing during his pilot courses. Falkowski secured protection of the texts he wrote by hiding them his mother. When the Soviets conscripted him, the pages of notes were hidden. Unfortunately and inadvertently, many of the bound notes fell apart and were destroyed. Sadly, the writer told me that he lost many nice stories.

Falkowski disclosed to me that, writing his stories in Polish came as an early decision at the start of his writing career. While in the army, the writer's fellow Polish comrades teased him for "writing something all the time". Possessor of everything "somewhere in his head", he wrote what he saw, what he heard, and what he thought.

Writing even during his evening drafting courses, he wrote after work while a career employee of the port of Montreal. Performing as a draftsman during the day, he wrote during the night. When having his evening supper he wrote, and later at the table, he sometimes fell asleep to wake up in the morning, still at the table. Confiding to me, he confessed that such behavior caused him problems with his health.

In Montreal, he began to rewrite everything anew. Disclosure of this monumental task was not revealed anyone. Never believing that his writing would be published, he confided in me that he had always written for himself for all those years.

Dreams? . . . he had various visions of both success and failure. Of course, he dreamed of being published. But when he thought of giving his work for appraisal, he reverted to the fear of making a fool of himself, afraid that no one would like his writing.

In May 1992, in polemic ardor concerning a certain case for which he had conclusive evidence in notes, he sent a letter with fragments of his journal to the Paris "Kultura" periodical.

Jerzy Giedroyc, the Editor, used them in issue 101 of the "Zeszyty Historyczne" (Booklets on History) quarterly.

Rudolf received two letters from the Editor.

21ˢᵗ June 1992
Dear Sir
Thank you very much for the highly interesting materials you have sent. I would like to use them in "Zeszyty Historyczne" titled "Poles, Red Army soldiers" (1940-1945)".

If you allow me, I would like to make some serious cuts to leave out some unnecessary insertions of political polemics. Obviously, I fully share your opinion on the politics of General Sikorski and the atmosphere in the Polish army in Great Britain, but I would like to compress the text more in order to avoid unnecessarily lengthy fragments.

Kind regards
Jerzy Giedroyc

2 nd July 1992
Dear Sir
Thank you for your letter of 29th June and for your consent to make the cuts. I will publish your article in the August issue of "Zeszyty Historyczne", which will be published by the end of August.

"One day from my journal" is written flowingly, it reads well, the only danger is that written in such a way, the journal might grow and expand into a giant machine. You would have to make a severely limited selection of the materials you have.

With the best regards
"Kultura" Editor
Jerzy Giedroyc

Rudolf Falkowski told me that he always missed someone who would encourage him, someone who would take an interest in his writing, but he was alone. As an unrecognized Polish hero, he never benefited from someone to talk to or someone to seek advice from. Once a Greek friend advised him to continue writing, saying he had a gift of observation.

> For all those years of my long life," Rudolf surmised, "I wasn't lucky enough to meet anyone who would want to listen about my life's passion and about my love for words . . . but I lived to see the moment.

The most important moment in Falkowski's life was meeting a man to whom he is greatly indebted.

Luckily, the aspiring writer finally managed to stumble across a person who not only listened to his story and not only read the accumulated volumes of paper, but who generously organized their rewriting, handled the editing and, finally, had the manuscripts published.

The person he owes so much to, whom he came to admire and whose friendship he now cherishes, was a great book lover from Montreal, Stefan Władysiuk—tall, handsome, with a dose of charming modesty, a historian by profession, and a graduate of Gdańsk University. Since 1985, Wladysiuk has served as the librarian in the Polish Library, 3479 Peel Street, Montreal.

"Stefan Władysiuk took my writing under his kind wing," Rudolf told me. "Stefan is calm and composed, very intelligent. He is my soulmate, he is like a brother to me."

Stefan also told me his only regret was that it didn't happen some twenty years earlier . . .

***

The published Journals were receptive to a positive opinion from Professor Jerzy Holzer, who shared it in the Warsaw "Polityka" weekly. A selection of fragments was published.[15] Holzer wrote e.g.:

> On occasion, he gave spontaneous negative comments about other nationalities—Ukrainians, Jews, Russians, Lithuanians, the British or the French—but he was sometimes also critical of some features of Poles. He was open and tried to understand the unfamiliar. Beside the descriptions of interesting and often lesser known realities, that is one of the major values of his journal.

***

Rudolf Falkowski elaborated to me about his novel written in English. Initially starting to write it in 1955, he corrected it many times since. Rudolf sent it to me. The story had no title, it was his second novel, and I liked it. I gave it to my husband, Norman, to read, and he was possessed by it. "It's a good novel; it would make for an interesting film," he said. "The typescript has some minor linguistic slips, I'd be glad to correct them . . . " Norman wrote a letter:

9 March 2010
Dear Mr.Falkowski:
I am writing to relate my experience in reading your book manuscript that I have taken the liberty to title "The Lady Investigator".
Aleksandra told me of your background, your exceptional military career as a pilot and your lifelong ambition to be a writer. Sir, in all honesty, you certainly have the talent!
Initially, I read the first three chapters of your manuscript during my after dinner reading period. My interest was immediately triggered such that I found myself reading a few chapters every day. This habit continued until I finished.
Your story of Captain Natasha Smirnova has a wonderful plot that captured and maintained my interest. The idea that the military investigator would have the responsibility to prosecute her former lover is a stroke of genius. Your story also reveals the mentality of the Russian Communist, his inhumanity and his fatalistic outlook on life. The flashback to earlier events in the lives of Smirnova and her lover provides a wonderful mechanism for maintaining a readers' interest. I might add the sexual portions of the story are tastefully done without an over emphasis that would diminish the basic military plot. Your description of the wonder of nature in Russia I also found very captivating.

I think you have written wonderful story that should be published! It would make a great movie as well. I would be very happy to provide a "polishing" of the text if it were available in a cleaner/unmarked version
Sincerely yours,
Norman Boehm

A few months later the electronic version of the book came to Norman. He sent it back after editing the language. He told me he (an American) learned much about the Russians and stressed again that it would make a great, suspenseful movie.

***

. . . What joins people and what makes them different? . . . Their dreams and their sensibility.

. . . Perhaps the story moves me so much because as a writer I think with tenderness and understanding of those for whom writing is a great passion. It seems to me that we belong to the same specific community, that we come "from the same cloud", as my niece likes to put it.

Two years before reaching 90, when Rudolf Falkowski saw his first book published, he was happy and gladly shared his joy.

He told me, "Now that I'm 90/91, my passion for writing is as great as it once was. I remember whole scenes that I'm writing about, I know what the end will be. I am a normal human who happened to live in a queer time. I have no secrets to reveal. But I do have journals, and they reveal concrete people and established facts."

***

When he reached 90, Falkowski repeated the same words he did when his first book was published two years earlier—that he would like to be... twenty years younger.

He died on 16th November 2012, at the age of 93.

The following announcement was published by the Polish Consulate in Montreal:

Rudolf Stanisław Falkowski, veteran of the Second World War, pilot and writer, has died.
We were sorry to learn that on 16th November 2012, Rudolf Stanisław Falkowski, veteran of the Second World War, and pilot of English and Polish squadrons, had passed away. He was a man who rendered great services to Poland and to Canadian Poles. He was buried in Kwatera Zasłużonych (Section of Honour) of the Polish Socio-Cultural Foundation at the Notre-Dame-des-Neiges Cemetery.

***

Stefan Władysiuk said that Rudolf Falkowski died a happy man. The two colleagues were discussing project for a new novel in English. With happiness, the author relished the interest that the two published books were receiving.

I cannot help saying that while he owed much to fate and to God, he also owed a great deal to the goodwill of his Montreal friend Stefan Wladysiuk, the man who helped him make the second dream of his life come true.

I too wish I were able to give him another twenty years of life.

***

Below are some excerpts from the journals of Rudolf S. Falkowski: [16]

Saturday, 5ᵗʰ September 1942, Blackpool
Today we received our RAF uniforms. Very similar to ours from before the war, just more steel in colour. Caps with an emblem—a crown over wings, and around the shield the words: Per Ardua ad Astra. Tony Z., from Oszmiana, my current mate, who was educated in a humanities class, trans-lated it to me: "Through adversity to the stars". My Mom once said that he, who reached for the stars, was a threat to the skies. So be careful with it.

A new era starts in our lives. We are told we are in a civilized, even elegant world, according to some. We shall see.

(. . .)
Monday, 22ⁿᵈ June 1943
Today we were visited by President Raczkiewicz of the Polish government in exile. We stood in a row. An ordinary car came. The first to step out was some General. Głuchowski? Wasn't that the former vice-minister for military affairs? The same who in Spring 1939 together with Kasprzycki dismissed the commander of air-power, Gen. Rayski, on charges of interfering too much in airplane production and complaining there weren't enough planes? I wonder what happened to Kasprzycki and Rayski. Meanwhile, another car came, without an escort, with a little white and red flag on the front right fender. The orchestra started playing the Polish anthem, and a tall, elegant gentleman in a hat stepped out of the car, without any escort; he looked like a president should. He reminds me of President Mościcki[17] with his stance. He went along the row of soldiers and from the end he slowly went back, shaking the soldiers' hands. He talked to us, asked questions: where are you from? How long it's been? And listened attentively. He exuded openness and familiarity; as if he were chatting with old friends over a pint.

The ceremony was nearly two hours. He bid his farewell with a loud "Czołem żołnierze!" (Goodbye, soldiers!) [18], to which we yelled "Long live the President!", and he left as he had come - alone.

It was only then we noticed a group of several officers and a few generals. Where did they come from? They had stood apart from the President, and he talked to none of them.
(p. 379)

Beside facts and recounts, there are also his own reflections and records of conversations. E.g. on Polish and Lithuanian women:

Saturday, 11ᵗʰ October 1941, "Komsomolets"
Again the evening conversation is about Lithuanian women—mothers and daughters. Those who were interned in Lithuania in September 1939 say that Lithuanian women are like Polish ones in character. Meaning? E.g. they are more overbearing, like to boss around, give orders, and are not too tolerant of "male foolishness", whatever that means. (. . .) But I like Maksymowicz's theory the best. He is from Lutsk, Volhynia, and I think he might be a Baptist (. . .) He often quotes various parables from the Bible. He says that a person's maturity depends on their Guardian Angel. He told us an interesting story about Jacob from the Bible, who dreamed of fighting with an angel. Jacob won and the angel never "mussed" him again. He decided that Jacob had grown and matured, and needed the angel no more. And that it is from there that our prayer comes—"Angel of God, my guardian dear, To whom God's love commits me here . . . ". So he claims that both Lithuanian and Polish women, and all Catholic women in general, still need their angels. And the women of the East are more reflexive; the Orthodox faith develops in them the sense of the third dimension which raises them—universal women, mothers of life—infinitely over the symbols of all religions. They mature quicker and their angels leave them earlier. (p. 281)

(. . .)
Thursday, 24ᵗʰ June 1943
Yesterday we had a visit from the Theatre Ensemble of the Polish Army. The local Lviv Merry Wave with their Tońkos and Szczepkos[19] performed. (. . .) Beside the Wave, two ladies were performing: Majewska and Mira Grelichowska.(. . .) Quite honestly, the whole event didn't make much of an impression on us. We were more interested in what would come after the show—would they be friendly like the President, or would they watch us from a distance, pointing fingers and saying: "Those are the ones from Russia". The Ensemble consisted of a large number of people, mainly women—young, pretty and elegant. And just like we expected, they started being friendly with the older people who are always loafing around here, and of course with the officers. We stood aside and didn't rightly know what to do with ourselves. Some of the ladies gave us sideway glances, but they were afraid to approach . . . lepers. (. . .) We were again displeased with the conduct of our

countrywomen. What perverse hypocrisy! Just like before the war, when they sang of handsome soldiers, but kept at a distance from them. We unwittingly compared those women to the nurses in Kermine and we saw a huge differ- ence. The nurses were women from the Polish Eastern Borderland. A differ- ent world.

"All that is the elegant Warsaw society. They sing of Lviv, while they've never been there and likely don't know where it is," commented one of the guys.

(p. 380)

A scene with a dog, with one of the few comments on Russians in the book.

Sunday, 22nd March 1942, Kermine
It was nearly 2 am. And all of a sudden, all car doors opened as if against one order, NKVD agents in the cars opened the doors from inside on one side and jumped out on the other. We rushed in a horde inside . . . and to the windows. A line of NKVD agents on each side of the train. The last car—the last squadron—was still getting loaded. They had a mascot, a large domesti- cated dog. The dog sat on the platform and just turned its head left and right, waiting for its turn. "Hop in!" I heard the last soldier say.

The dog was already on the stairs when a heavy paw of an NKVD agent fell on its neck, yanked backwards, and the dog somersaulted back to the platform. "Sobaka ostajotsa (The dog stays)," the agent raised his hand in warning. He surely expected the owner to react. He slammed the door shut. The train started moving. The dog jumped to all fours and jumped to the closed door. The heavy paw grabbed its neck again. We helplessly watched the dog's tragedy from the open windows of the last cars. When the last car passed the platform, the dog tried to break away again. Then a flash from the gun. The dog curled up, and thus we left it.

We pulled our heads back inside. We were sitting as if in a daze, without one word. I had never seen anything like it before. And while during my whole stay in the USSR I really had never had any trouble from its inhabi- tants, I suddenly realized in what sort of country I was living. I only felt my stomach cramp. (p. 343)

He wrote little complimentary of the British. He believed that "*If you don't smash the German or the Brit in the face, they're never going to be your friends.*"(24th May 1942) (p. 371)
He included a drastic observation on how the British acted towards Poles.

Sunday, 8th June 1947, Keevil
One more thing, vulgar, unseemly to write of, but we've come upon it before. Farting, to put it in vulgar terms, for you cannot find a delicate

expression for that. Farting towards us. At first we thought that maybe they'd eaten something not digest able and they had to break wind. Happens to anyone. But we realized they did actually do it on cue. Each time when a friend of our commander dropped in for a chat, the British greeted each other like dogs, raising one leg and . . . poof! And they even commented to each other, "Ah, it's a good one!"

One day an African-American soldier joined us. We noticed that each time he heard the noise, he seemed to curl up in embarrassment and whispered something under his breath. Was he that delicate? Or did he hear it so many times before that he knew what such behavior meant? He surely knew enough on the subject, but due to our ranks he was afraid to say anything aloud. Finally, Sakiewicz asked him if the conduct of the British is supposed to shows their respect for people outside of their race.

"Yes, sir," confirmed the man. "They got bored with such as I long ago. You are new. The whole station knows what you are doing here. Their dogs have more tact." (p. 645)

***

The description of the Poles farewell with the 303 Polish Squadron is deeply moving.

Sunday, 1ˢᵗ December 1946.

On Thursday, 27ᵗʰ November, the commander of the Squadron took the 303 Squadron badge, the shield with the American flag, the crossed Kościuszko scythes, off the Mustang's cabin. Quietly, calmly, no fanfare, no tears. It looked like degradation—tearing off the shoulder straps, the buttons, breaking the sword on the knee. Well, perhaps not as dramatic, but close.

By the evening, the mechanics tore the badges off the rest of the aircraft. We said farewell to arms... and went to supper. We finally knew exactly where we stood.

Yester night, Saturday evening, there was a general farewell party. The news reached Norwich quickly, and this time there came two truckfulls of young ladies with golden hearts and eyes open for a good party. The company raged full time, had a fill of drinks, a natural thing. Around nine some sauntered back to their barracks and came back about an hour later, this time without scratches on their muzzles or dishevelled hair.

In England, just before leaving for Canada, Falkowski wrote:

Sunday, 2ⁿᵈ November 1947
Lucky are those who are to be shipped to the States or to Canada. Those who go to the States get the highest recognition. When it comes to Canada, you always end up hearing the States are better, anyway.

The book ended on his arrival in Canada:

Sunday, 4ᵗʰ April 1948
*Fourth day out in the sea. The last three days, I barely stood. (. . .) We
reached Halifax early morning on the 8ᵗʰ April (. . .) Place booked on the
train. Along the windows, limbs of leafless maples and mighty spruces with
traces of clotted resin. Two squirrels chasing each other on the tree trunk
suddenly stopped opposite the window and threw interested looks inside. The
train set off at five pm. Four days and five nights before I reached Alberta,
and that is only three fourths of Canada's width. Well, after crossing Russia,
wide spaces don't make much impression on me anymore.*

NOTES

1. Currently Ivano-Frankivsk, Ukraine.
2. In 1919, Podolia was in Poland. Currently it is part of Ukraine.
3. Hanka Ordonówna, Ordonka (1902-1950) – highly popular Polish singer, dancer and actress. In 1931, she married Count Michał Tyszkiewicz. In 1939 arrested by the Germans, on her release she left for Vilnius, where she was later arrested by NKVD and taken to a gulag in Uzbekistan. Released as a result of the 1941 Sikorski-Majski agreement, she organised help for orphans of Polish deportees into Russia. Evacuated with the orphanage to Beirut, she stayed there until her death of tuberculosis.
4. Horas non numero nisi serenas – I don't count the hours unless they're tranquil/bright/serene.
5. Tadeusz Romer (1894-1978) – Polish diplomat and politician, Poland's ambassador to Italy, Portugal, Japan and the Soviet Union, later Minister of Foreign Affairs of the Polish Government in Exile (1943-44). From August 1940 to November 1941, he managed to get transit, asylum and immigrant visas to Canada, Australia, New Zealand, Burma, Palestine, the United States and some Latin American countries for two thousand Polish-Lithuanian Jewish refugees. After the war he settled in Canada.
6. Eastern territories of Poland during the interwar period, with such major cities as Lwów (Lviv) or Wilno (Vilnius). Today, the area is divided between Western Ukraine, Western Belarus, and southeastern Lithuania.
7. Sovkhoz– state-owned farm, usually contrasted with kolkhoz, a collective-owned farm. While the latter were created by combining small individual farms together in a cooperative structure, a sovkhoz was organized by the state on land confiscated from former large estates, and was on average nearly three times larger than a kolkhoz. The employees were paid regulated wages, whereas a kolkhoz distributed the farm earnings among its members.
8. See: Lynne Olson and Stanley Cloud, "A Question of Honor. The Kosciuszko Squadron. Forgotten Heroes of World War II," Alfred A. Knopf, NY 2003.
9. Korpus Ochrony Pogranicza (KOP) – Polish military formation (1924-1939) created to defend the eastern borders against armed Soviet incursions and local bandits, separate from the regular Border Guard which controlled the other borders.
10. What you write with a pen, you can't hack away with a hatchet.
11. Spoken words fly away, written words remain.
12. Ramparts of the Holy Trinity or Okopy Svyatoyi Triytsi, currently Okopy, Ukraine.
13. Stanisław Skalski (1915-2004) – Polish fighter ace of the Polish Air Force in World War II, awarded the Distinguished Service Order and the Distinguished Flying Cross. Czesław Miłosz (1911-2004) – Polish poet, prose writer, translator and diplomat. 1961-1998 a professor of Slavic Languages and Literatures at the University of California, Berkeley. U.S. citizen since

1970. In 1980, awarded the Nobel Prize in Literature. Karol Modzelewski (born 1937) – Polish historian, writer and politician. Imprisoned for anti-communist views, interned during the martial law in Poland (1980s), member of Solidarity.

14. Władysław Gomułka (1905-1982) – Polish communist activist and politician. Leader of post-war Poland until 1948 and then again 1956-1970. Edward Gierek (1913-2001) – Polish communist politician. Replaced Gomułka as First Secretary of the ruling Party in Poland. Wojciech Jaruzelski (1923-2014)- Polish military officer and politician. First Secretary of the Party 1981-1989, Prime Minister 1981-1985 and Poland's head of state 1985-1990.

15. *Dziennik pilota* (Pilot's Journal), "Polityka", 23rd October 2010.

16. Rudolf S. Falkowski, "Żużle na dłoni," Montreal 2007. ISBN 0-9692784-5-4.

17. Ignacy Mościcki (1867-1946) – Polish President 1926-1939, the longest serving President in Poland's history.

18. The traditional military salutation "czołem" serves both as a greeting and a farewell.

19. Wesoła Lwowska Fala – at first a weekly radio program of the Polish Radio Lwow, composed mostly of light music, sketches and humor, one of the most popular programs of the Polish Radio between the world wars. After the outbreak of the war most of the artists were mobilized into the Polish Army and successfully evacuated from Poland. They served as the Wesoła Lwowska Fala Theatre on various fronts of the war.

Among the best-known comedians associated with the Merry Wave were the Szczepko and Tońko duo, known for their ragamuffin dialogues in the Lviv dialect.

Chapter Three

"I carried the films on my head"
Photographer of the Warsaw Uprising

Wiesław Chrzanowski

For my book *Kaia, Heroine of the 1944 Warsaw Rising* I needed pictures showing the Uprising. Cezaria Iljin Szymańska [Kaia, pseud.] contacted me about a friend of hers, saying I would have "the most beautiful pictures from the Uprising", that he'd made about 150 of them. She showed me a postage stamp with a soldier in position in the ruins of an orthodox church in Podwale and said it depicted Jurek Sikorski, pseudonym "Sikston", from the "Anna" company. The picture had been made by Wiesław Chrzanowski. The Polish Post issued two stamps with his pictures. The other one, from mid-August 1944, shows the shooting post near the Castle Square, between Piwna and Ślepa Streets: MCpl OCdt Jerzy Sikorski shoots the Błyskawica submachine gun left-handed, with Cpl Jerzy Łyczkowski standing nearby.

I had noticed Wiesław Chrzanowski's pictures some time before that. My father had an issue of the "Stolica" weekly of 1st August 1957 in his collection. It was dedicated to the 13th anniversary of the outbreak of the Warsaw Uprising and showed a dozen pictures made by Wiesław Chrzanowski. Other pictures came from: Eugeniusz Lokajski, Stanisław Sommer, Zbigniew Brym, Wincenty Szober, Irena Skotnicka, Jerzy Świderski, E. Świderski, PSW[1] "Majer", PSW "Joachim", PSW "Małgorzata", Elżbieta Łaniewska.

Wiesław Chrzanowski is one of the photographers whose pictures are included in the album issued by the Warsaw Uprising Museum, titled *(Roz)poznaj Warszawę. Nieznane fotografie zbiorów Muzeum Powstania Warszawskiego (Know Warsaw (Again). Unknown Pictures from the Collection of the Museum of the Warsaw Uprising)*[2]. The pictures concern not only the Uprising, but war-time Warsaw in general. They had been made by 42 photographers, and only a few of whom had actual education in the field[3]. Also included are single pictures by a German soldier, Hans Joachim Goerki, and an American journalist, Julian Bryan. The album shows over two hundred pictures, which beside documentary value carry a huge emotional impact. In the pictures, the insurrectionists fight, rest, bury their dead. Sometimes they look straight into the camera, e.g. some of the soldiers leaving the city to go into captivity. For the viewer, their looks are most moving.

In 2005, Norman and I visited Halina and Wiesław Chrzanowski. They were living in the Wola district on Żytnia Street made famous by an Uprising song "Pałacyk Michla Żytnia Wola" (Michler's Palace, Żytnia Street, Wola). In the pictures from the Uprising, the tall, straight-backed host looked like Rudolf Valentino, the handsome star of silent films known to the pre-war generation.

He showed us pictures from the Uprising—all were remarkable.

Wiesław Chrzanowski's photographs are the only ones to show the fight of one battalion chronologically, especially of the "Anna" company, from the start to the capitulation day. They show people resting, eating, the ruins, various views on the tragic events of those days, e.g. evacuation through the streets of the destroyed city, as well as portraits of their friends.

I was very impressed with his stories and with the pictures. I told him I would like to write about him. He was happy to hear this news. I was finishing another book then, but we kept in touch, as I came to Poland twice a year. Wiesław and Halina visited me in my flat in Warsaw. He brought with him the book *Bataliony AK „Gustaw"-„Harnaś" w Powstaniu Warszawskim w fotografii Wiesława Chrzanowskiego* (*"Gustaw"-"Harnaś" Battalions of the Home Army in the Warsaw Uprising in Photographs by Wiesław Chrzanowski*).

I made notes from our conversations. I asked him among other subjects about the cameras he used. We talked of having a series of meetings. Another time when I called, Halina said, "Wiesław is not well, he forgets a lot and his condition is deteriorating rapidly . . . " Half a year later she told me he didn't even remember what had occurred on 1st August 1944.

In April 2011 came news of his death.

I was sorry that we could not have talked more, that we hadn't had the time to prepare a more comprehensive story. From my notes, I reconstructed what I'd written, and I also incorporated materials he gave me.

People sometimes mistake his name with Wiesław Chrzanowski who was an MP and a Seym Marshal[4]. The latter was also a soldier in the Warsaw Uprising, but he was not a photographer and didn't take beautiful pictures from the Uprising.

Wiesław Chrzanowski, of Nowina family crest, was born on 4th December 1920 in Sosnowiec. He remembered his early childhood on 14 Piłsudski

Street, in a house with a large garden that had fruit trees, gooseberry and currant bushes, and vegetables. He had two older siblings: sister Hanna[5] and brother Jerzy.[6] When he was seven, his parents Teodor and Zofia moved to Sopot, which was then within the Free City of Gdansk[7]. His father worked in the Gdańsk Shipyard. Wiesław attended primary school in Gdańsk, commuting from Sopot, as he remembered, in a one-car school train with a combustion engine. Three years later, in the Autumn of 1930, the whole family moved to Warsaw to live on Aleje Ujazdowskie. Wiesław went to the eight-year Joachim Lelewel's gymnasium in 53 Złota Street. In the third grade, he joined the 5th Warsaw Scouts' Team. He liked sports: skiing, swimming, springboard and platform diving. The school also had military training. In the seventh grade, he went with his friends at the end of the school year to a camp in Lidzbark, where they also had a sports competition. He took first place in discus throw and received a diploma. On graduation, after passing the final exam, on 20th May 1938, remembering, it seemed the world stood open for him and his friends. He played tennis for a few weeks, then vacation ended. The graduates were conscripted, and he went to the Sapper Reserve Officer Cadet School in Modlin near Warsaw and became a member of a bomb-disposal team that consisted of only twelve soldiers. In the September Campaign, he and his comrades defended the Modlin fortress.

Since 1940, Wiesław Chrzanowski belonged to the underground National Military Organisation (Narodowa Organizacja Wojskowa—NOW; in November 1942, it became part of the Home Army). During the Nazi occupation, he was trained in the underground Officer Cadet School, studied in a two-year State Higher Technical School at the Warsaw University of Technology (taking at the same time parallel clandestine classes following the study program of the pre-war University).

For two years before that, he'd had a steady friend, Hanna Dragatówna. He liked to describe her "Waikiki beauty type". He kept her picture, with an inscription in the back: "Never forget me, dear Wiesio—Hanka. Warsaw 25th December 1938".

20-year-old Hanka was killed in Auschwitz in 1941.

Halina Borczykówna, called Dziusia, from the Juliusz Słowacki's gymnasium in Warsaw was an acquaintance. She was the fiancée of Jerzy Wojno, an armour officer cadet. On 18th September 1939, her fiancé was mortally wounded in his tank as he was defending Warsaw in the Wola district. He died in the hospital, never regaining consciousness.

Wiesław and Halina became friends and spent time together. They also both shared the experience of losing their loved ones. He visited Dziusia in her house in Narutowicza Square, and Dziusia visited the Chrzanowskis in their house on Wilcza Street.

They were engaged on 4th December 1942. Wiesław gave her a ring which had belonged to his grandmother, Jadwiga Różycka. Dziusia gave him a silver cigarette case with an engraved inscription.

The life around them was difficult. Twice he escaped a street roundup—*łapanka*[8]. He remembered various images throughout his life . . . for instance, the time when on his mother's names-day, 15th May 1943, he took a picture of the burning Jewish ghetto from the window on the fourth floor, by Three Cross Square.

***

1st August 1944

Wiesław remembers well that at 9 a.m. a liaison courier came to him with the order to come at 11:30 to 27 Żurawia Street, flat No. 5. Commanders of the "Gustaw" battalion company were to be briefed, and Wiesław Chrzanowski was appointed the commander of the flame thrower platoon.

He took his bike and some food. He had much to do before the "W" hour, the starting time, which was set for 5 p.m. He saw Dziusia, who had come to Wilcza Street. Both comforted his mother that the Uprising would be short. They were full of enthusiasm and faith. They said goodbye to each other. Little did they know that they would not see each other for nearly four years.

He remembered that their order for five flame-throwers had not been executed. For six days, he was a liaison officer for the battalion commander. In the Old Town, he was deputy commander and then commander of the 2nd platoon, "Anna" company, "Gustaw" battalion—until the end of the Uprising. He received a Home Army armband and an identity card. At first the soldiers wore the armbands on the left arm, but since some German units also wore their armbands on the left arm, an order was issued to wear theirs on the right arm.

The battalion was quartered for two days in the Raczyńskis' palace, and then later in house No. 1 on Kilińskiego Street,. On leaving the Old Town, on the 5th September, going down Czackiego Street towards Świętokrzyska Street, Chrzanowski was injured by a gunshot in the right leg. He spent two days in bed in the flat of his sister Hanna in Wilcza Street. A few days later he rejoined his company.[9]

63 days of combat ended with a capitulation.

Years later, he said he'd come to the conclusion that human life of a "fair starting level" depended on two factors: geopolitical situation and mere coincidence. He gave some examples of situations from the Uprising in which he'd taken part.

" . . . On 1st August, our unit mobilized in Senatorska Street. On the next day, I went to the information point in the yard of the house No. 13 in Leszno Street (today 93 Solidarity Avenue). At the opposite side of the street stood (and still stands) a Protestant church with a soaring tower decorated with sculpted leaves. On 4th August, in the evening, I stood in the street before the gate. Suddenly I saw the flash of a fuse of an artillery missile being shot. The shrapnel missed me entirely, but the missile hurt and killed many dwellers of that big house who were praying at a shrine built in the yard, i.e. 10 meters behind my back."

***

" . . . On 13th August, in a room at the ground floor of the right outbuilding (3 Kilińskiego Street) perpendicular to the street, in the bed there Ludwik Gawrych, commander of the "Gustaw" battalion lay wounded, in his dark blue, bloodied suit (he had been injured in an attack at the school on Żelazna Street, at the corner of Leszno). It was hot. Flies walked over the bloody stains. A young boy rushed in to report that our men seized a tank and it was standing in the street between 1 and 3 Kilińskiego Street. I was sitting on the floor, and two others ran out to see the "marvel". Ludwik said to me, You're a sapper, check that tank over . . . I got up and at that very moment the blast of a detonation threw me against the wall. But for 10 seconds, I would have been next to that "tank". The tank had actually been a man-driven armoured carrier of heavy 362 kg (798 lbs) TNT charges meant mainly to destroy bunkers.

" . . . Barbara Potempska, wife to 2nd Lt. Sławek, had been standing with a friend by house No.1. She was thrown face-down to the ground, the explosion tore nearly all her clothes off, save for shoes and garter belt. Three small shrapnel lodged in her right cheek, and were never removed. Her friend virtually disappeared, nothing was left of her. But I saw a human shape affixed to the wall of the Raczyńskis Palace, about the first floor. They found a few heads in the Market Square. Two other personnel from "Gustaw" who ran out ahead of me, I didn't see the remains of either. The front walls of houses 1 and 3 were pressed inside at the first and second floors. The owner despaired, but she was comforted to see a pillow lying in the ruins and she wanted to take it. I told her to leave it because it wasn't a pillow. She touched it and fainted. It was a naked abdomen, not bleeding, cut off evenly at the groin and at the ribs. A cut-off foot stood on a window sill, and on the remnants of the window frame, there hung intestines, draped like a curtain . . . "

***

" . . . I saw what a hot blast could do when I was in the hospital in the Raczyńskis Palace, 7 Długa Street. I came to see a friend who was dying when they brought in a group of five people. Their hair was packed with earth and straight as a pin, and skin was hanging off their fingers. That had been done by the "cow"—a missile from a grenade launcher—of the blast type. Their condition was the result of powerful hot air pressure exploding in a walled-in room somewhere in the Market Square."

***

" . . . On 16th August, three days after the explosion on Kiliński Street, our 2nd platoon was defending the Piwna-Podwale zone. One of our men came up to report that the Germans put a "Goliath" in the corner of the barricade and the house (the even side). "Goliath" differed from the previously mentioned vehicle in that it was not man-driven, but directed by cable or through radio control. I ordered everyone from both sides of Podwale to withdraw and to put fire underneath the vehicle. The explosion brought down many walls of houses in Podwale and Ślepa Streets, which had already been ruined by bombings. I instinctively dropped to the ground, but a three-brick piece fell from above the third floor and hit the middle of my back. An X-ray made later (in Germany) showed it had damaged two thoracic vertebrae. Another brick brushed against the Achilles tendon in my right leg. I walked with a cane for a few days. Years later, the damage to the two vertebrae extended to other ones."

***

" . . . I think it was on 20th August that I went with 2nd Lt. Jerzy Siwiec, called "Jur", to the odd-numbered side of Podwale to the Evangelical consistory, to see if it was possible to use the building with its high ground floor—having a full flight of stairs—for defense. A few minutes later, we heard the sound of approaching Stuka bombers[10]. For cover, we stood in the open door to the stairs, where the wall was the thickest. There came a sudden roar and the air went black with earth and soot. For that, we had scarfs made of flowered flannel. When the soot thinned some, at the end of that flight of stairs we saw a 35-kg bomb, a misfire, lying on the ground. Within five seconds we were on the opposite side of Podwale. The Germans sometimes used bombs with delayed ignitions, you know, but this one was a misfire."

***

" . . . On 26th August, the Germans launched a massive attack on our positions at the western edge of the Castle Square. Aircrafts, tanks, "cows"[11] and infantry. Our defenders withdrew some 50 meters (164 feet). After that hell, 2nd Lt. Wojtek Sarnecki, 1st Lt. Jerzy Lewenty and I—three platoon commanders of the "Anna" company—went to see the effects of the attack. We went from Ślepa Street through some garage to the yard of the house in 6 Podwale Street. We quickly learned that the Germans had seized the area and threw a grenade at us, probably a concussion one. The result was that the blast tore my pants down the inner seams! The pants became a skirt . . . We drew back. They threw three more grenades, but those were defensive (fragmentation) ones. Since then, the defense line remained withdrawn to that point until the end of the combat in the Old Town. But perhaps that first grenade was a fragmentation one, too!"

***

"In Śródmieście Północne, the Germans regularly fired mortars at two crossings of Jasna Street interchangeably: the corner of Świętokrzyska Street, then Moniuszki Street. Four of us ran in a row, ten meters apart. After getting through Świętokrzyska Street, we waited for the explosion at the corner of Moniuszki Street and then we were off southwards. As we ran through the street, an unexpected shot came into the very place. I was running last. The shell hit the ruins of a tenement on my left and rolled down a steep pile of debris. Running, I leaped over the misfire rolling under my feet."

***

" . . . I think those five examples (I'm not counting the blast "cow" and bricks falling on my back) are enough to prove my philosophical thesis. During the whole Uprising, I was saved from serious injury at least seven times."

***

GERMAN CAPTIVITY

Wiesław was a POW in the camps in Fallingbostel, Bergen-Belsen, Grossborn, Sandbostel and Lübeck. After the capitulation of the insurrectionists' units, he was taken to *stalag* XI-B in Fallingbostel. His POW No. was 1396. He recalled years later:

"We were marched out in close-order columns to captivity, having shed any German uniform elements, on 5th October. We went as the 3rd battalion of infantry regiment of the University Cadet League [12]. The sad act of giving up our weapons took place in Narutowicza Square. We had hidden the better weapons in the cellars in Krucza Street, and the guns we gave up to our captors were intentionally damaged, but they were still our weapons.

"We went 17 kilometres to Ożarów, to a cable factory, and two days later we were transported in freight cars through Berlin and Hannover to *stalag* XI B (Stalag= Stammlager—basic camp) in Fallingbostel.

"Half of the camp was a concentration camp, and the other half held Soviet POWs, but that half bore little difference to the concentration camp.

"The Germans did not abuse us, but the main problem was hunger. I ate salt, it helped. Before Christmas, we were given one American package each through the Swiss Red Cross. Conditions for trade got better, since the soaps, chocolate and American cigarettes could be exchanged for bread from the guards.

At the end of November, the Germans set up a camp for women from the Home Army near our camp. We could see it behind the wires. Just before Christmas, the women were taken to Oberlangen.

"On 22nd January, we went back to Fallingbostel, and from there we were taken in freight cars to *oflag* II–D in GrossBorn, about 60 km north of Piła (called Schneidemühle by the Germans). A huge camp, it imprisoned over 2 thousand Polish POWs from the September Campaign. On 28th January, the whole camp was evacuated due to the advancing eastern front. One of our friends somehow obtained a German map and some copying paper, so I copied part of the map, thinking they would take us to a train in a day or two. To make sure, we made 3 sleighs from the plank beds, each to hold eight men. In Bergen-Belsen, we lived in a 24-person room and kept together.

"The march started in the winter at -18 degrees Celsius, (0.4 degree Fahrenheit) and the first night was the worst for me and the others, as we had no shelter from the cold. I had officer boots of very thin leather, and as I went through the snowy dirt roads, the snow on my boots melted despite the freezing weather and my socks were wet. It was not a dream. My boots froze solid, I was 24 years old and didn't even catch a cold. We walked like that for 850 km to Sandbostel (*stalag* X-B) near the Dutch border.

"We stayed there for a week. About 7th April, the Germans took us (500 officers from the Bergen-Blesen camp) 150 km to *oflag* II-D near Lübeck. But it was Spring already.

"*Oflag* II-D near Lübeck (a Hanseatic city with a white and red flag, like the Polish one) consisted of abandoned barracks of a motorized army—numerous garages and two huge blocks. We slept in a block on a few hand-fuls of straw. Lübeck was one of the centers for dispatch of American pack-ages, and as the German transport wasn't good, we were given a package every few days."

***

I took pictures of my mates

"In the *oflag* in Lübeck, I drew a few scenes from our journeys. I was given some remains of watercolors from a Polish POW and made a few pictures in color.

"We were liberated on 2nd May about 4 pm by the British Army of the Rhine (BAOR). An hour before that we heard their artillery and saw smoke over the city. Our camp was located near the Lübeck-Travemunde (lit. mouth of the river Trave– into the Baltic Sea) highway, five kilometres from Lübeck.

"On the next day, 3rd May, we organised a celebration of the Polish national holiday [13]. Everyone came to the assembly square, including foreign-ers, mainly the British. The Polish flag was hoisted and then we had a Mass."

***

In captivity and right after liberation I took 52 pictures

"As in Lübeck, the Poles experienced some friction with the Germans, and we were moved to nearby villages, northwest of Hamburg, in Schleswig-Holstein. Together with about 50 other officers, I was quartered in emptied houses in the village of Lentforden.

"Since the liberation, I sent out dozens of letters to various charity organisations, to the Red Cross in Poland and in Europe, searching for my fiancée, Dziusia.

"On 5th October, I received a message that she was in Sweden. Halina had been in three concentration camps, and had been released from the last one, Ravensbrück. With a group of other prisoners she was taken to Sweden, within the operation of Count Folke Bernadotte (of the Swedish royal family), who obtained Himmler's consent to free 25 thousand women from concentration camps, including 4 thousand Poles from the Ravensbrück camp. [Some of them were brought to Sweden - AZB]. We started writing each other. The British would not give me a permit to go to Sweden.

" . . . As I was walking down the street in Lübeck, I saw my brother Jerzy at the railway station, who had come from London in his uniform. My brother took me to Brussels, and he returned to England. I decided to return to Germany, and started studies at the Technical University in Munich, which was located in the American zone.

"For some time, I was active as the commander of the 2nd company in the Polish Work Centre (POP), unloading food transports. There I met the commander of the 1st company, 2nd Lt. Stanisław Zybała[14]. I was given an American uniform, a living facility and pay. Both shoulder straps had "Poland" sewn on them. The Polish Work Camp was dissolved."

***

He received his diploma from the Technical University in Munich on 11th August 1947 with top grades. He remembered that his thesis was for some years a topic of students' practical classes.

Wiesław returned to Poland in November 1947. He stayed with his parents in Chorzów, and mid-September 1948, he returned to Warsaw, where he stayed with various people. He married Halina (Dziusia) on 16th September 1950 in Warsaw. They had a daughter, Marta, who later graduated from pharmacy studies. She is married to Grzegorz Ławniczak, with whom she has two daughters, Anna and Dorota.

At first he worked in the tractor factory in Ursus, in the mechanical department. He left after a month and was accepted at the Institute of Precision Mechanics (IMP). At the same time, he was hired—at first part-time— as the Senior Assistant Lecturer at the Warsaw University of Technology in the Chair of Metal Processing, Faculty of Mechanics and Technology. In total, he worked for 32 years at the Warsaw University of Technology, where he took his doctoral degree in 1975 and later further academic degrees. In the Institute of Precision Mechanics, he worked for 43 years, until 1991.

He proudly said:

> . . . For long years I have promoted the ethos of the Warsaw Uprising. The issue of the "Stolica" weekly of 1ˢᵗ August 1957 was dedicated to the Uprising, and my pictures were included[15]. In the albums: *Miasto Nieujarzmione (The Invincible City)* and *Dni Powstania (Days of the Uprising*; both published by IW PAX). In the historical treaty *Powstanie Warszawskie (Warsaw Uprising)* by Adam Bartkiewicz (1964). *Przemarsz przez piekło (Marching Through Hell)* by Stanisław Podlewski (1971). I don't know all the books that contain my pictures. I think there are about 40. I organised individual exhibitions in 1984 in the Polish Tourist and Sightseeing Society (PTTK), Old Town Square, and in 1994 in the Museum in Leszno. The Polish Post used my pictures in two stamps.

I asked him about his cameras and how he kept them safe during the Uprising

After the Uprising, the house where Wiesław Chrzanowski had lived was burned down. The preservation of many pictures, and even negatives from pre-war times, that he protected in storage can be considered an exceptional feat.

In August in the Old Town, and in September in Śródmieście Północne., 145 pictures of the Uprising were taken with 33-mm Kodak Retina and Kine Exakta cameras, using e.g. Agfa Ultrarapid, Agfa Isopan F, Agfa Isopan ISS and Mimosa negatives. Some of the undeveloped films he hid in a cellar of a house in 3 Wilcza Street, the rest he managed to smuggle into subsequent POW camps. In captivity—in Bergen-Belsen and Lübeck—he took over 90 pictures with Exakta.

When I asked about his first camera, he recalled it had belonged to his father: a Carl Zeiss-Jena "Computer". He said:

" . . . the focus was set on the focussing screen, but with a stand, with the possibility to regulate the lens's position horizontally and vertically with screws, and most importantly—with an automated shutter (from 1 to 1/250 sec) and regulation of the lens's diaphragm."

The camera was not burned in the Uprising. Wiesław kept it, and it was fully functional. He used it for micro-pictures, i.e. pictures in large close-ups.

His father had given him a Kodak camera, which he used during the Uprising. As he described it, "The focus was set by turning a ring with a distance scale. Its drawback were the negatives: a file of 12 film pieces 6x9 cm, divided with black paper. When pulling out the subsequent screens, you pulled the film in the back of the camera in position for pictures."

In the Old Town, he borrowed a Retina camera. In Śródmieście he had a Leica (f/3.5)[16].

I asked how he protected his camera. The answer amazed me:

" . . . To the camp, I smuggled the Exacta camera, two rolls of non-exposed film (including one in the camera) and some of the undeveloped films from the Uprising. *I carried the films on my head, under my cap, and the camera in a map pouch hanging on my back.*

" . . . We were searched three time in the five camps, in total. The most detailed search we had in Bergen-Belsen. The Germans told us we would be moved to a different camp. In reality, once we packed, we were all brought to the "walks" part and after a detailed search conducted right by the gate by three guards at the same time, we were led back to the barracks area. Everything had been turned upside down in the barracks, even the pallets were torn open. Faced with such a search, 2nd Lt. Henryk Ożarek quickly let them search him, and I put the camera and films in a German map pouch and threw it over the heads of the guards, the fence and the closest barrack, like a discus, right to Henryk who was already waiting there. The camera (more precisely, the film shifting mechanism) was damaged. I didn't have the conditions to repair it until we got to the 5th camp, Lübeck."

When I asked him in 2006 what camera he had now, Wiesław Chrzanowski said:

"In 1995, I bought a Japanese Yashica camera. It does everything by itself."

Halina Borczykówna, later Chrzanowska

In the Uprising, Halina (born 16th September 1920 in Warsaw) at first prepared meals and brought them—often under enemy fire—to the soldiers in the trenches and on barricades. She told me:

" . . . I never spoke to anyone about it before, you are the first one, Aleksandra . . . I was in the "Juliusz" special unit of the Home Army in the Ochota district. We helped collect the wounded in our sector. I have that image in my memory . . . I was carrying a wounded insurrectionist on stretchers with a friend. The Germans shot high, lighting the area. We saw a wounded man lying in the grass . . . He had an open wound of the abdomen, his internal organs were visible. He was crying and begging to be shot. We went a bit further with the stretchers, and my friend stopped. He turned back and shot the man."

***

"After the Uprising ended in defeat, the insurrectionists and civilians were brought to Pruszków near Warsaw. A large crowd of people walked in a long, sad row. Warsaw became a desolate, ruined city [17].

"From Pruszków, people were taken in groups to various camps. Some tried escaping, some successfully. For instance, my sister, Danuta, also a Home Army soldier, put on a white coat with a white-red flag badge and she managed to smuggle herself and other people outside of the area closed off by the Germans in Pruszków. We weren't together, so she couldn't help me.

"People also escaped on the way, when the train stopped, they jumped out and didn't return.

"The people they took away—Uprising soldiers and civilians—were locked up in so-called labor camps. The Germans used the prisoners for various labor, e.g. to clear the area of debris after bombings of the Allied Forces.

"Briefly, at first I was in Woldenberg, then Ravensbrück, then Bergen-Belsen, and back to Ravensbrück. The camp was for women (but there were also children), established back in 1939. The women worked hard in special production halls, many (called "guinea pigs") had medical experiments conducted on them: bone and muscle surgeries, bacteria injections. They also died of hunger, cold, exhaustion, illness. They were murdered individually and in groups. In particular, mass executions concerned women from the Polish resistance movement and Jewish women. By the end of 1944, a gas chamber was built, where about 5-6 thousand women were killed.

"I was in a group which included 10 German women. I was the youngest, they ranged from 30 to 50. I asked one of them why she was in the camp. She said that the Germans arrested everyone who was part of a religious sect— this was what they called e.g. Jehovah's Witnesses. She said they were particularly abused, sent to do the hardest work, made to "give up different thinking". Those German women were kind to me, almost protective.

"Once when I was ill, I went to the Czech woman who was in charge of the block and said I was feeling unwell, that maybe I could go to the hospital. The hospital was a barrack with plank beds, actually, serving as a hospital. She showed me the barrack: it had beds with dying people, barely moving. She told me to try and hold out.

"We were told to go to various barracks to collect those who were seriously ill. They were brought to a special unit, undressed and put on a large pile—body on body. The women were alive—they were emaciated, weakened, exhausted, but they were alive. They asked us to leave them. They begged for help in Polish, German, Czech . . . they begged for mercy. Those are such terrible images, and as I grow older, it is harder and harder to put them aside. I remember their legs with traces of experiments conducted on them, whole bodies were often covered with injuries. I remember all this in such detail . . . I wake up at night and the pain inside is unbearable.

"What I saw in Ravensbrück still invades my dreams. I was in a group which cleaned the barracks of the "guinea pigs". Some of them were lying there very ill. I remember two girls, 16 and 17, who were awaiting their turn for experimentation, and they managed to escape the fate, because the war came to an end. Only the two of them survived. One of them was my friend's cousin.

"Once they brought in French women . . . What they did, their behavior, that shattered my image of French women. I still cannot recover from what I'd seen.

"In all that, we hid two Jewish children, a 7-year-old boy and a 10-year-old girl, in the last barrack, No. 32, where the "guinea pigs" were. We managed, despite constant searches, to hide them and keep them covered as necessary. When an inspection was made, they weren't found. They survived.

"I was in Ravensbrück until April 1945. About that time, as a result of negotiations conducted by the International, Swedish and Danish Red Cross (the above mentioned Count Folke Bernadotte took part in those negotiations), about 7500 prisoners were taken to Sweden. They included Poles, and me among them.

"And so I went to Sweden. We were first brought in freight cars to Denmark and then by ship to Malmö. It was there that news of the war's end reached us. I went to school, learned Swedish, then worked first as a nurse in a hospital for the released camp prisoners, and later in a weaving factory.

"I can still communicate in Swedish. But I don't really like that nation. For the whole war, they helped Germans and traded with them, made lots of money by doing so. Well known is the fact that they let the German army pass through their country on their way to attack Norway. They guarded railway tracks when trains with German soldiers were coming through, so no harm would come to them.

"Many people immediately returned from Sweden to Poland. I was hesitant. News reached us about arrests of Home Army soldiers, about sending some of them to the East, deep into the USSR. I heard that Cezaria Iljin (later Szymańska), Uprising [Kaja, pseud.], who went to see her family in Białystok, was arrested there and sent to the NKVD camp in Ostashkov, Russia. I was afraid to return, but finally made the decision. I obtained a passport and a reciprocal visa. They thought I would go for a visit and return to Sweden.

"It was October 1947. When I got off the Gdynia-Warsaw train, I didn't recognize my own mother. She was 47, and looked to be 90. Thin, emaciated, hunched over. My father died in Woldenberg, and Mom went through several camps, including Neustadt Gleve.

"I lived with her in our former flat in Narutowicza Square, with other people quartered with us. We lived in one 15-square-meter room, with another family living in the other one.

"Mom never recovered from what she'd been through during the war. She died in Warsaw at 62 years of age.

"I married Wiesław in 1950, but we were no longer the same people as eight years earlier when we became engaged. We had not seen each other for nearly four years and although we wrote each other, each of us had gone individually through different ordeals, each of us had seen and lived through much grief and misery. We had changed, and those experiences didn't bring us closer. We had our own pains, our own tragedies, scenes we remembered. I didn't ask him about his, and he never asked about mine. We were in a way alone with our experiences. Wiesław knew where I'd been, but he didn't know what I went through.

"Wiesław saw people die and suffer, but he found great support in the asset of graduating summa cum laude at the University in Munich. After the war he worked at the Technical University and the Institute of Precision Mechanics, he was fulfilled professionally. I liked my job as an editor in the Project Office, but for long time I have hurt, and I still do.

"My daughter Marta and granddaughters (Dorota and Anna) are a great joy to me. I even have a great-granddaughter, Paulina. My daughter and granddaughters have studied, graduated, and are living their own lives. I come from "a different era", I was raised differently. And I have my traumas.

"The images of bodies of very ill people, naked, which I carried with the others to put on the piles, have haunted me for years and now they only come back stronger. I am unable to push them down into the furthest recesses of my mind. So many years have passed from the war, and those memories still haunt me at nights."[18]

NOTES

1. Polowy Sprawozdawca Wojskowy – Field War Correspondent.
2. Warsaw 2009.
3. Antoni Bohdziewicz [Zetka, pseud.] Sylwester Braun [Kris, pseud.] the Ruegers: Halina [Małgorzata, pseud.] and Leszek [Grzegorz, pseud.].
4. Wiesław Chrzanowski (1923-2012) – Polish politician, founder of the Christian National Union party (ZChN), lawyer, Polish Seym Marshal (parliament speaker) in 1991-1993, Minister of Justice and general prosecutor (1991).
5. Hanna Chojnacka, photographer, after the war lived in Katowice.
6. Jerzy Chrzanowski, engineer, after the war emigrated to the United States.
7. Wolne Miasto Gdańsk (Free City of Danzig) – a semi-autonomous city-state that existed between 1920 and 1939, created in order to give Poland access to a well-sized seaport. It included the city of Gdańsk and other nearby towns, villages, and settlements. It was separate from post-World War I Germany and from interwar Poland, but not an independent state.
8. Łapanka – a widespread Nazi German tactic used in occupied countries, especially Poland, whereby German military forces ambushed at random thousands of civilians on the

streets. The civilians were captured in groups of unsuspecting passers-by, or kidnapped from selected city quarters that had been surrounded by German forces ahead of time. People caught in roundups were most often sent to slave labor camps in Germany, but also taken as hostages in reprisal actions, imprisoned and sent to concentration camps, or executed in numerous ethnic cleansing operations.

9. The injury healed up only in 1946, i.e. two years later.

10. Junkers Ju 87.

11. That was the name given to German launchers by Polish insurrectionists.

12. Legia Akademicka – voluntary student military formation established 1918 in Warsaw, later reformed into a regular infantry unit; reactivated 1929 and later 1937.

13. On 3rd May, 1791, the Constitution of May 3 (the first modern constitution in Europe) was proclaimed by the Parliament of the Polish-Lithuanian Commonwealth (a dual monarchy comprising Poland and Lithuania). The document was seen as proof of successful internal reform and as a symbol promising the eventual restoration of Poland's sovereignty, but it remained in force for less than 19 months. By 1795, the Partitions of Poland ended the existence of the sovereign Polish state for 123 years. Norman Davies described the document as "the first constitution of its type in Europe"; others have called it the world's second-oldest codified national constitution after the 1789 U.S. Constitution.

14. A chapter on Stanisław Zybała is included in my book "Dreams and Reality. Polish Canadian Identities", Toronto 1984, pp. 85-97.

15. I write about that above.

16. He said that years later, in Germany, he bought a Leica with a Summitar lens (f/2).

17. From all Warsaw districts, a total over 15 thousand soldiers of the Warsaw Uprising (including 6 generals) was taken into German captivity. 11,668 of them went through the Ożarów camp, the others through the camps in Skierniewice and in Pruszków.

See: Warsaw Uprising insurgents in German POW camps, prepared by Maciej Janaszek-Seydlitz, transl. by Ewa Bultrowicz: http://www.sppw1944.org/powstanie/powstanie_oboz_eng.html

18. Halina Chrzanowska passed away on October 3, 2016. Her second granddaughter, Małgorzata was born in July 2017.

Chapter Four

Varsovians in the States

Krystyna and Marek Jaroszewicz

They were born in Warsaw.

They met as youngsters at a manor in Gulbiny, Pomerania, and later became friends as young people in Warsaw. The beginning of World War II in 1939 separated them. Krystyna served as a messenger for the Polish forces during the Warsaw Uprising.

They met again—miraculously, in their own words - in Zurich, and it was there that they married. After the war, they settled in the United States, and Marek became one of the most outstanding American architects.

Marek often said he'd like to do architectural design for Warsaw, and that it was a city he thought of with concern and love, and gladly visited, even though the visits grew less and less frequent with time. During his visit in 1999, he died suddenly.

And so he stayed in Warsaw.

They are both buried in Powązki, the major Warsaw cemetery.

The pair were particularly elegant, open-minded, kind, and took a humane interest in others. I believe everyone felt well in their company. In the nearly twenty years that we knew each other, there were a few several-day-long meetings, regular telephone calls, letters and notes. We shared news on what was currently important for us at the time.

American distances—one who hasn't experienced them cannot imagine them . . . We were living in different states: Krystyna and Marek in Florida, and I in Texas and also in Delaware.

Zofia Korbońska[1], a friend of Krystyna since they lived in Warsaw, now resided in Washington DC. Both ladies, Krystyna and Zofia, became very close people to me. I learned much from them, due in part to the fact that they had varying opinions on Poland and the United States.

I visited Krystyna and Marek Jaroszewicz in Gainesville, Florida, with my then teenage son, Thomas. A few years later, while studying architecture at the Warsaw University of Technology, my son had to move to the States to be near me. Marek recommended the 5-year architectural course offered at the University of Arkansas in Fayetteville. The university offered teaching by the great architect E. Fay Jones and others. As part of the curriculum, the students spent one semester in Rome.

I also visited Krystyna and Marek in Gainesville with my husband. With the visit, Norman joined the circle of friends of the couple, who attracted people with their openness.

In the book *Amerykanie z wyboru i inni* (*American by Choice*), I included my interview with Marek Jaroszewicz on architecture (I reprinted it in *The Roots Are Polish*[2]), titled "Co-Author of the International Charter of Machu Picchu". But our conversations went beyond the interview in the book.

Krystyna and Marek, casual and friendly, gladly shared their experiences. I learned about their lives and their opinions on immigration, Warsaw, Poland and America. Both had led an uncommon life, and have certainly enriched mine with their friendship.

***

KRYSTYNA BRZEZICKA (LATER JAROSZEWICZ): GULBINY, HRUSZOWA, WARSAW

Krystyna said she had a sad childhood, mainly due to her parents' divorce. A five-year-old girl then, she was deeply affected by it. She and her sister Barbara lived in Warsaw in the home of their father, Mieczysław Brzezicki. Raised by their grandmother, the girls were neat and trim, they went to the seaside each year, but they lived a sheltered life, they missed their parents, and were aware of it. They spent their summers with a cousin, Lila Brzezicka, who was raised by a French governess in the estate of Gulbiny, which belonged to Helena and Bolesław Brzezicki[3]. The estate lies in Pojezierze Dobrzyńskie (Dobrzyń Lakeland) in the district of Rypin, on Lake Długie.

There she met Ewa and Jaś Jaroszewicz, siblings, who later organized soirées in Warsaw. At one of them, she met their cousin and her future husband, Marek. All her life, Krystyna believed the manor house in Gulbiny had to be the most beautiful Polish manor house that one could ever imagine, with a "classic" porch supported by four columns. Lilac bushes reached through a window into the dining room.

The manor had a magical quality about it that attracted guests. The first owner of the manor was Alojzy Piwnicki. In the 1820s, young Fryderyk

Chopin, later a famous Polish composer and pianist,[4] visited and played there. In her book about him, Zofia Jeżewska quotes Chopin's letter to his parents: "Sunday we were in Gulbiny, visiting with Mr. and Mrs. Piwnicki..."[5]. In 1939, Gulbiny hosted General Władysław Anders, who was later to become the legendary commander of the Polish Armed Forces in the East and of the 2nd Polish Corps, which he commanded in Italy (Battle of Monte Cassino and Battle of Ancona).

Krystyna Brzezicka told me that in Gulbiny she learned to ride horseback and spent some of the most memorable summers of her youth. Other summers spent in the eastern Borderland of Poland, in Hruszowa, Polesie were also interesting for her. The estate belonged to Maria Rodziewiczówna[6], a writer related to the girls' mother, Zofia Weichert-Brzezicka.

After the last summer of 1939 - Krystyna saw neither Hruszowa nor Gulbiny ever again.

***

Krystyna Brzezicka was born on 28th November 1922 in Warsaw, and all her life she had a special emotional connection with the city. Her most poignant memories come from the time of... the Nazi Occupation. She met and made friends with many great people, developed her mind, participated in underground activity, which was an important time for her, one that impacted all her life. She liked to stress that there was no party, no ideas to divide people, there was one enemy to unite everyone. During the Occupation, the society was uniform, united, with one aim motivating everyone.

She attended one of the best and oldest Warsaw schools, Cecylia Plater-Zyberkówna's school (founded 1883), and took her high school graduation exams in Miss Jakubowska's clandestine classes in 1941. Young people grew up quickly. She said during that time, learning was viewed in a special way: it was forbidden, so everyone who learned was aware of the significance of what they were participating in. During the Occupation, social life also went underground, and so did many cultural events. Meetings with discussions on literature were organized, poems were read, books were discussed. Krystyna remembered once being taken by Rom Wańkowicz, son of Witold and Marietta, to visit his aunt Zofia, who lived on Dziennikarska Street in the district of Żoliborz. She'd met Rom during summer holidays in Zakopane, in 1939. At the meeting in Żoliborz, where young people regularly met for afternoon teas, she met Krysia, the older daughter of the great writer Melchior Wańkowicz.[7] Such meetings usually had some eight to ten participants.

Participants included future Nobel prize winner, poet Czesław Miłosz,[8] who read his poems, and Jan Strzelecki, later to become an outstanding sociologist, who shared his impressions on reading philosophical texts.

Krystyna Brzezicka was younger than everyone else, and she remembered she wasn't at her most comfortable in such company. Everyone made the impression of being wiser and more knowledgeable than she. They had long fervent discussions, made plans of who would live what way and who would do what in life.

Joining the civil underground activity like most of her friends was natural. She was a liaison officer in the Government Delegation for Poland[9] of the Polish Ministry of Foreign Affairs. After her house was searched, her superiors told her to leave Warsaw for a time. She hid in Kraków, in the house of her uncle Eugeniusz Brzezicki, a professor of psychiatry. She compared the atmosphere of the two cities and noted that Kraków had a different mood to it. It made the impression of a city of depressed people, but life was easier, food more plentiful. She thought Warsaw had a bolder, more patriotic atmosphere to it. Krystyna visited landed estates, met her school friends. At that time, she saw the great support and aid of the gentry for the partisans.

SOLDIER OF THE HOME ARMY —
NURSE IN THE WARSAW UPRISING

In January 1944, she returned to Warsaw and was recruited to the Home Army. She trained as a nurse with the 1st Light Cavalry Regiment. Since the winter of 1940, Krystyna had been working in the Polish Red Cross as a secretary to Maria Tarnowska[10], Vice-President of the Executive Board of the organization and a person whose conduct left a permanent impression with Krystyna. She then worked for Maria Tarnowska until the outbreak of the Warsaw Uprising. Countess Tarnowska, descended from the Sviatopolk-Chetvertynsky princely family, prisoner of the infamous Pawiak prison in 1942, was a major of the Home Army. She was respected even by the enemy. By the end of the Warsaw Uprising, she negotiated to have the insurrectionists considered soldiers, she took part in capitulation negotiations and in talks concerning the evacuation of civilians, as a result of these efforts, 20-25 thousand people were able to leave Warsaw between 8th and 19th September 1944.

When the Uprising broke out on the 1st August 1944, Krystyna was a nurse with the 1st Light Cavalry Regiment, within the Baszta Battle Group Regiment. She remembered going with her friends from her barracks on Czerniakowska Street through the Sadyba neighborhood, up to the Hospital of the Sisters of St. Elizabeth in Mokotów district and the Gąsecki pharmaceutical factory on Belgijska Street. By the end of the Uprising, she journeyed with others through the sewers from Mokotów to the city center. They wandered around, came up to the Szucha Alley[11] a few times and had to return. They wandered through the sewers for sixteen hours. She came out through a manhole at the corner of Ujazdów Avenue and Wiejska Street by the Three Crosses Square. By the manhole, her sister Barbara and a friend, Maryjka Grocholska (later Wąsowska), were waiting for her. Barbara had managed to find somewhere a pot of water, so

Krystyna could wash her face, but still she couldn't see for two days afterwards. Not much later, she learned that many of her family and friends had died.

.... On the 15th July 1942, Jaś Jaroszewicz, Ewa's brother, was killed as he was returning from an operation in Vilnius. A member of the first military underground organization, and later of the Union of Armed Struggle (ZWZ) and then the Home Army, he was first in the Baszta Regiment, and then moved to the Wachlarz Sabotage Organization within the Home Army. He and his friends Jerzy Miecznikowski and Feliks Dunin-Karwicki died while being raked with gunfire in a burning car.

.... Rom Wańkowicz [Knut, pseud.] was killed in the storming of a German bunker in Mokotów, on the first day of the Uprising.

Later, his uncle Melchior Wańkowicz wrote that Rom's mother searched for his body a long time. When he was recognised among the exhumed bodies, Melchior's wife Zofia did not let her sister-in-law come close. "After all, they had been buried for half a year. She [Zofia] knelt down to wrap a blanket around the body in a rotting jacket, the jacket he received before the Uprising and was so proud of, and in the knee-high boots which he liked so much to show off . . . " [12]

... Krystyna Wańkowicz [Anna, pseud.] Melchior's daughter and liaison for the "Parasol" scouts' battalion, was killed on the sixth day of the Uprising during the battles at the Calvinistic cemetery on Młynarska Street.

***

KRYSTYNA BRZEZICKA

She liked to talk with me about that time, glad that I was listening attentively and that I understood. She spoke of her reflections—she recalled the Warsaw Uprising as the only and greatest time to dispose of any thoughts about yourself. Never in her life, before or after that time, did she have such an attitude or see people with such attitude towards themselves and towards others. You could not say "I'm scared", for the fear could have spread to others. The unwritten law was to behave so as to mobilize others. She spoke with utter conviction that the ties among the people you spent those times with were stronger than any other, and lasted all your life.

She also said that scenes from the Uprising returned in her dreams for the rest of her life.

***

She left Warsaw with a crowd of other evacuees, heading for the nearby village of Ursus including sister Barbara and cousin Elżbieta who journeyed with her. The evacuees were taken in train cars near Auschwitz. The train stopped at the siding of the Auschwitz station. They waited the whole day.

When the train was turned back and headed towards Wrocław, there were loud prayers and great sighs of relief.

She didn't say much about those days after the Uprising. The memories were still fresh and still painful.

Some years later, I read the memoirs of an insurrectionist of the Warsaw Uprising, Tadeusz Olszewski, pseudonym "Siwy", from the "Kiliński" unit[13]. To quote a fragment: "Later in Ursus trains came in. We'd slept for a day or two on concrete. The Nazis obtained railroad cars and took us deep into German territory. We stopped near Auschwitz, in the Szczakowa camp . . . We were afraid they might take us to Auschwitz . . . There, they deloused us, we had to undress completely, there was a steam bath . . . For two days we travelled in stock cars. I remember going (still during the day) through Wrocław (the Germans called it Breslau), we stopped (our train with the prisoners, everyone, civilians) at a railway embankment and there was an air raid. The planes flew above our heads, and the train stood there. We looked on, there was good weather. We could see the allotment gardens near Breslau . . . We stayed in such camps for a few days each time. We were quarantined, there were steam baths, we walked among the wired fences. [The conditions] were awful. Imagine sleeping on bare planks. These were supposedly plank beds, but bugs dropped on your head. Bedbugs, thousands of them. You felt something dropped on you. Couldn't touch it, it was so disgusting. We knocked them down. After all the delousing they put us in a camp with a mass of bedbugs. . . . .There were no shelters, so you ran [from the air raids] wherever you could."

She explained briefly that they were deported to a camp in Germany. She said she managed to escape the camp and she went, mainly walking, through Silesia, the Sudety mountains, and Austria . . . there she stayed for two months, working in the Zilberschoff estate. She then went to Southern Germany. She headed for Switzerland, knowing that Marek was there. She even sent him a postcard from Bavaria.

In April 1945, she managed reach Switzerland, where she was immediately interned.

Like I said, she spoke only briefly about the escape and the following months, about that time. She said it was difficult to think of it, but that various images returned in her dreams now, after so many years. Such dreams brought back the fear, the insecurity, the suffocating trepidation.

When I asked about Warsaw, about Poland, she said she thought about the Uprising with great pain—that it all failed, that she had to leave, wandering into an uncertain future. That like others, she lost everything.

THE WINTERTHUR CAMP IN SWITZERLAND

After reaching Switzerland, immediately, she was interned and placed with a group of other refugees from Germany in the Winterthur camp near Zurich.

As she stood among the throng of people of various nationalities who stayed in the same camp for the interned, a question was asked whether anyone spoke French. Madame Dunant had come, the granddaughter of Henry, founder of the Red Cross. Krystyna came forward, and she showed Madame Dunant around the Buren camp. The Madame, endeared with Krystyna's conduct and her fluent French, helped her get a job in an office of Aide Suisse a la Pologne in Bern, a charity organisation helping Poland (1945-46).

At Winterthur, it turned out that Marek was also there.

As it happened, in the Winterthur camp she asked the physician who was examining her whether he knew of a Marek Jaroszewicz. And he did know him!

They met twelve hours later.

Meeting someone who was both dear to her and whom she'd known in the good old pre-war times, was a major event for her.

She also spoke of other feelings.

Her contact with the West for the first time in her life, in those circumstances, was very sad. That was the word she used: sad. She knew some door had closed, something was irrevocably lost.

She was speechless with the beauty of a new, different landscape, and amazed with what seemed like a different morality of people, who had not experienced war and who were now—as she put it years later—"fighting the interned".

***

MAREK—SON OF WŁADYSŁAW JAROSZEWICZ

Marek Jaroszewicz was born in Warsaw on 12th June 1921. He came from a well-known family, whose members were Piłsudski's supporters. Marek's father, Władysław Jaroszewicz, born in 1887 in Baku, a chemist, was an activist of the Piłsudski supporters' camp and a Government Commissioner for the Capital City of Warsaw. Marek's grandfather, Bolesław, had worked in oil production in the Caucasus as an engineer. His wife was Amelia Honwalt.

The family moved to Voronezh, then to Kiev, where Władysław Jaroszewicz graduated from high school in 1906. He then studied mining engineering in Liege, Belgium, and later chemistry in Kiev University. After studies, he worked as a representative of coal companies in the Donets Basin as mine director, and since 1917 was head of the board of the Southern Donetsk Coal Company. He was an active member of the Polish Military Organisation[14]. In January 1919, he came to Warsaw to work in the Treasury. Closely involved with Piłsudski, he quickly advanced and carried out various assignments. During the 1920 Kiev Offensive[15], he was in Ukraine as a delegate of the Ministry of Foreign Affairs for economic affairs. Beginning in July 1920, he held the function of a civilian commissioner under the command of the North-Eastern Front for some time. In 1926, after Piłsudski's successful May Coup d'État, and in succession of General Sławoj Składkowski, Jaroszewicz was appointed Government Commissioner for the Capital City of Warsaw. He was thus head of e.g. the police and press censorship.

Marek was an only son of Władysław Jaroszewicz and Zofia Hulanicka (in 1939 his father remarried his new wife Janina Kalicka). Zofia Hulanicka (1895-1956) was a pianist. She gave concerts all over Europe, and went to Switzerland often. She was the only woman accepted as a student by the famous Polish pianist and composer Ignacy Paderewski.[16] She learned foreign languages, and spoke Italian and Spanish fluently.

Until he was eight, Marek had his own private tutor. When he was eleven, his parents divorced, and he stayed with his father, who sent him to a school for talented children, a gymnasium founded by the Sułkowski princes in Rydzyń. The school had a high educational level and rather strict discipline. Marek remembered that they'd already been taught function differentials for three years before final school exams. He was a temperamental boy. For a drunken scuffle in which a professor was hit, he dropped out of school. With the help of the then minister of education, Tadeusz Łopuszański, he was placed in the Stefan Batory gymnasium in Warsaw and took his final exams in 1938.

He decided to study at the mechanics faculty of the Warsaw University of Technology, but when it turned out he'd failed the entry exams, he joined the Anti-Aircraft Artillery Officer Cadet School. He was given a temporary leave due to a leg injury sustained when skiing in January 1939. Not to waste the time, under the persuasion of his friends (among them Maciej Nowicki, who later became a famous architect) he took preparatory courses for architecture. He then passed the entrance exams (there were 700 candidates for 70 places, as he remembered and stressing his success as he spoke to me) and became a first-year student of the architectural faculty of the Warsaw University of Technology. Yet he never started his studies.

Upon the outbreak of the war, Marek worked for free as his father's secretary in the Government Commissioner's office. As directed by the Prime Minister Felicjan Sławoj-Składkowski, Władysław Jaroszewicz oversaw the evacuation of the Government from Warsaw to Romania. He went with his son at the head of the column, which set off on the 17th September 1939. They drove slowly, taking the back roads, usually with their lights off.

Marek decided to join the Air Force. Together with a group of Polish pilots he took a ship through the Red Sea, the Bosphorus, the Dardanelles, Constantinople, Cyprus, Haifa, Malta to Marseille, and there they took a train to Lyon. For two weeks they stayed in the aircraft base in Bron. Here he was told he hadn't been admitted to the air force. He left for Paris, where he enlisted in the newly created Polish cadet school. He was sent to Coëtquidan, where he was assigned to the 2nd Rifle Division under the command of General Prugar-Ketling (General Duch's 1st Grenadier Division). There he made friends with Ksawery Pruszyński, as well as with the ex-ambassador in Berlin, Józef Lipski. Marek joined a reconnaissance platoon, with which he reached the Swiss border. On crossing it, they were disarmed by the Swiss and interned in Winterthur.

ARCHITECTURAL STUDIES IN SWITZERLAND

Not much later, the Polish Government in London signed an agreement with Switzerland to allow younger people to finish their studies. On passing the entry exam, Marek was accepted to the architectural faculty. There were 25 people from Poland, and he remembered Jan Gundlach from Łódź. The lectures were in German, which he knew from his classes in Rydzyń high school. He remembered that he and a few friends who spoke the language translated the lectures into Polish for the others. Through that repetition, he learned. He graduated in January 1945 as the second best among forty three students. Swiss authorities pondered whether to acknowledge the diplomas. In the end, the diplomas were exchanged for Swiss ones, of the Swiss Federal Institute of Technology. The Poles had a right to work, but only if there would be no Swiss applying for the particular job. Three fourths of the salary was to be deducted as repayment for the studies.

He lived in the camp for the interned in Winterthur and commuted daily by train to nearby Zurich, where he was working in a small architectural office. The salary was modest, and he earned some extra money playing the piano in a cafe in the afternoons, from five to nine.

In April 1945, he met with Krystyna Brzezicka in Zurich. They'd corresponded in the beginning of the war, and he also received her postcard from Bavaria, but he didn't know what happened to her later. They both consider that meeting a sign of destiny, as it was practically a miracle.

***

He wanted to have time for Krystyna, wanted to be with her for at least a week or two without outside influences. Yet the head of the architectural office where Marek was working did not want to agree to give him a leave, so Marek quit.

They married in Bern on the 18th August 1945 and immediately thereafter went for a trip through Switzerland and France. As an officer of the Polish army, which was part of the French army, Marek was entitled to French citizenship and he considered settling down in France. Yet he and Krystyna decided to go to America.

Marek's father, Władysław Jaroszewicz, went from Romania to England, but he didn't continue his political career there, and left in 1944 to the United States. He became a co-owner of a small orange farm in Florida.

He persuaded Marek to come with his wife to the United States. He promised to pay for the trip, and if they didn't like it there, he would buy them return tickets to France. On 24th April 1946, the couple traveled from Paris to New York by plane. In New York they took a train and after 24 hours they were in Florida.

Krystyna said that mentally she felt better than in the previous places. She realized she was in a free country, in normal conditions, where you paid for the ticket and could go wherever you wanted.

After daily reporting to the police in Switzerland, where she was always reminded she was interned and could not stay permanently, the new free life was a relief. When she was leaving with a ticket to America in hand, the previously unfriendly and disapproving Swiss clerk changed, became practically attentive. She told herself that if she ever went back there as a tourist, she would stay in a hotel and ring the bell for a maid to come and serve her . . .

. . . She worked later for eight years in the Detroit branch of a Swiss line, travelled a lot, mainly to Switzerland. She managed the Swissair office in Detroit (1958-63), then the European department in S&H Travel (1965-73). I never asked if she had ever kept that promise to herself . . .

When she came to the States, she was seven months pregnant. At the airport, their personnel graciously pulled up a chair for her to sit down, and served her without waiting for her turn. They said, "Good luck to you in this country" . . .

She was moved and bewildered, and filled with immense gratitude. In Europe she'd felt that they wanted to get rid of her.

Marek asked the clerk where they should report. "Nowhere," the man said and added, "We hope everything with you will be o.k."

To get a warm was a relief welcome after so many humiliations, when people in Europe wanted to just get rid of them. They stayed with Marek's father in Fort Pierce, north of Palm Beach. A week later, Marek visited a local architect, the only one in the city, and the man said he could hire Marek right away. Marek sent out his application to six architects further away, and all offered him a job. He chose Miami.

They felt uncomfortable in Florida, however, mainly due to the tropical climate. The air conditioning wasn't as widespread then, and they couldn't tolerate the heat. Krystyna didn't carry the child to term, she lost the baby, felt ill all the time, and stayed in the hospital frequently. Marek's father was taken ill—he was diagnosed with lymphatic cancer. Six weeks after the diagnosis, on the 5th June 1947, Władysław Jaroszewicz passed away.

Krystyna and Marek decided to leave Florida. They went to New York, where Marek looked for work for several months in vain. American soldiers returning from service were given precedence. They then went to Detroit, having been persuaded to come to Michigan by a friend, Januszewski, a wealthy Pole, owner of the "Dziennik Polski" daily, a printing house and a brewery. They stayed in a small hotel. In the telephone book, Marek sought out addresses of architectural companies, and among them found the company of the famous Finnish architect Eero Saarinen [17], whose work he'd heard of back in Switzerland. Twice, Saarinen refused Marek's application for a job, but the third time he extended a job offer himself. It was 1949, and Marek had already won a few awards.

The work with Saarinen became the foundation of Jaroszewicz's whole professional career. He worked there only four years, but the work was intensive and creative. Saarinen's company was at that time one of the most interesting and successful ones in the world.

Eero Saarinen, son of Eliel, who was also an architect, lived in the United States since 1923, where he studied at Yale University. After graduation, he first worked with his father, then independently. He designed mainly industrial buildings. His designs were functional, had innovative constructions and used modern construction materials. He was also involved in designing furniture. Working intensively, also on the weekends, Marek started to have problems with his health. He changed his job then, and became the chief designer at Victor Gruen Associates. He remained friends with Saarinen until the latter's death in 1961.

Like he said, he started his career by working 70 hours a week. Once, back in Fort Pierce, someone told him: "In America the difference between job and career is like the difference between 40 and 60 hours a week." But the results were impressive: Marek Jaroszewicz was counted among the top fifty architects in the whole United States.

In 1958, he opened his own architectural firm, but it didn't achieve financial success, and he withdrew from it. He started working with others, cooperating with such companies as: Vicot Gruen, Eberle Smith, Smith Hinchman and Grylls, to name a few. His next career plan, as he recalled, was to transfer his architectural career into the field of science.

He was first a dean at the University in Detroit (where he became a professor of architecture), then at the University of Michigan (where he taught design), Oklahoma State University (where he was director of architecture). For ten years since 1976, until retiring, he was a dean of the University of Florida in Gainesville.

The University of Florida is among the best American universities. The university ranks as the ninth largest in the States, and also ninth as concerns the number of students. The position of the dean of architecture was advertised as a broad responsibility, encompassing the faculties of: architecture, urban studies, landscape architecture, interior design, construction school). Seventy nine candidates applied, including eight from Europe. The application of Marek Jaroszewicz was interesting for many reasons. He had experience in renown companies, his own practice, many publications, many awards and top positions in competitions, he spoke foreign languages (French, German, Polish, English—fluently, and Spanish, Italian and Russian—well). He was accepted.

Under his management, the architectural faculty in Gainesville became one of the major ones in the whole United States. His students turned out to be top of Harvard classes. At an architectural convention, it was stated that out of fifteen people admitted to Master's thesis defense at Harvard, five came from the University in Florida headed by Professor Marek Jaroszewicz. He was the dean and also the teacher of practical architecture. His ability to make decisions and his experience as an active architect gave him an advantage over typical scientists.

His articles were published among others in "Architectural Forum" (New York), "Architectural Record" (New York), "Progressive Architecture" (New York), "Kokusai Kentiku" (Tokyo), "L'Architecture d'Aujour'hui" (Paris), "Bauen und Wohnen" (Zurich), "Werk" (Zurich), "Domus" (Milan), "Swiat" (Warsaw).

Many of his projects were published in major specialist journals in the States, Europe and Japan. He was a registered architect in Michigan, Ohio, Oklahoma and Florida.

He received many awards, e.g. from the American Institute of Architects, and the Association of Enterprise Architects in Michigan. He was also awarded the golden medal of the Florida Association of Architects, the highest distinction of the association he chaired in 1985.

He designed churches, houses, offices, primary and secondary schools, universities, dormitories, banks, motels, restaurants, libraries. For the design of the huge *Central Plaza* mall in Canton, Ohio, he received a local and a national award.

His name was listed in Marquis "Who's Who in America" (since 1978), "Who's Who in the World" (since 1982), "Who's Who in Technology" (since 1984).

He presented a paper in Lima, Peru, at the "Meeting of Great Teachers of Architecture" conference in December 1977. He travelled across the whole of Europe, the United States and Canada, and visited many countries in South America. Invitations to give lectures in international centers in the whole world, meant many travels to Europe, but also to Guatemala, Mexico, Saudi Arabia, Cameroon, or Colombia. Marek was a member of the American delegation to the 14th world convention of architects in Warsaw in 1981 and one of its twelve executive board members, and later co-authoring the Warsaw Architects' Declaration.

Earlier, he co-wrote the famous Machu-Picchu charter, which won the main prize of the Jean Tschumi International Union of Architects in 1978, and which was translated into over twenty languages. Marek translated the text from the original Spanish version into English, then it was translated into other languages. The charter was added to the Athens Charter of 1933, whose main author was Le Corbusier.

In Warsaw, when it was learned he was co-author of the charter, his fame grew, and he became particularly popular. The Poznań University of Technology invited him for a series of lectures; as well as by universities in Wrocław, Kraków, Gdańsk and Białystok. During his lectures, he showed slides, talked of Saarinen's work, about teaching and working in the States, and also about his own views on architecture.

***

Professor Marek Jaroszewicz held a very high opinion of Polish architects. He emphasised that they won competitions all over the world—in Milan, Rome, Madrid (first prize for the opera), and in Switzerland. Americans do not know of those successes, because they concentrate on their own area and achievements.

When he came to the States, Poland was a country little known. When he said he'd been born in Warsaw, he got polite answers like, "Oh, you are from Poland? Oh yes, my father visited Budapest during the war . . ."

The Smithsonian Institution in Washington organized a series of lectures on "Celebrated Capital Cities". They included e.g. Paris, Madrid, Rome, Berlin, Washington, Tokyo. The series was opened on the 17th October 1984 by Marek Jaroszewicz. He spoke of Warsaw, and started by saying:

I shall speak of a city where I was born and grew up until I was eighteen. The Second World War forced me to leave it. (. . .) . . . I will give you a view of my city—its life and its spirit. However, it is not an easy task without presenting the geographical setting and without giving historic context of the tragic but beautiful Polish history.

In his presentation, Marek Jaroszewicz went back to the oldest of times to move to the events of the last war. He said among other things that Poland defended itself longer than France. He spoke of rebuilding the capital after the war, showing 130 slides. He later repeated his presentation in Oklahoma.

***

When I asked him how he viewed his life, Marek Jaroszewicz said he believed himself successful, in his understanding of success and career. He lived his life the way he wanted, interesting, dignified, he always had a successful life. In academic spheres, he was a respected teacher, and his name was known and highly regarded. He also believed that to an American's understanding, where the measure of success is a lot of money, he was not such a successful man. He never made a fortune, didn't live in a residence, but in a pleasant, comfortable house.

For a long time he'd thought he'd return to Warsaw and help rebuild the city. However, the decision to stay abroad erased those plans. He said that the decision to stay abroad warped your life, that in a way, it rebounded onto you the rest of your life. He stressed that he believed himself a political immigrant, while all who came after 1956 he saw as economic immigrants.

He also said that he realized that despite the success he achieved in the new country, despite professional and personal fulfilment, he knew he was "alien". He had a different sense of humor, for instance, but he appreciated the element of habit. He appreciated feeling good and comfortable in the new country.

In his view, the immigration community was society viewed in a distorting mirror, a microcosm of the Polish society—it stressed the positive features, and the bad ones intensified, as well. Immigration had all the features of Polish people, but they were exaggerated, sometimes downright grotesquely so.

An English friend married to a Pole, Jean Uniechowska, who learned Polish, said, "I learned that if Poles are comfortable, they bitch about and badmouth each other, and when they're bad off, they offer hot soup to warm you up . . . "

Marek remembered a time when the whole Polish community in Detroit supported each other. They felt close, felt needed, they formed a force against the outer world, the alien, different reality. The Jaroszewiczes had a spacious house in Detroit at that time, and it was a particular haven for many Poles. After they left, there was no such house anymore. They organized Christmas Eves with nearly all their friends, sang carols together. When they were leaving Detroit, there were 65 people at that last Christmas Eve.

As instructed by the Headquarters of the Home Army in London, Krystyna established a branch of the Home Army in Detroit. Until she left in 1973, she was a member of the board of the Association, which was helping many families of soldiers, widows, and orphans in Poland. In Detroit, they organized literary meetings, lecturers were invited. Those included among others Zbigniew Brzeziński[18], Ambassador Józef Lipski,[19] or Congressmen Thaddeus Machrowicz.[20] For the 40th anniversary of the Warsaw Uprising, an image of Our Lady of the Streets, patron saint of the Uprising, was built at the American Częstochowa in Doylestown, Pennsylvania. Krystyna took an active part in preparing and executing the project.

***

"I had an interesting life, but I would have preferred to work in Poland."
Marek said:

"America is neither better nor worse. It is simply different, and you have to get used to it. Going to China, seeing slanting eyes, different clothing, you expect people to react differently than us. In America, even though people look the same as we do, the difference is the same as you would expect when travelling to China. I think the southern American states resemble Poland more, as concerns people's characters.

"I value America because it gives full personal freedom, you are free of any social rules and regulations. (In my youth, in Poland everyone was cautioned: this or that is not becoming, not appropriate . . .) I like the freedom of travelling, the spaces. . . . .At the same time, that personal freedom in the States sometimes smacks of anarchy.

"When I was young, I was nearly weighed down with my father's authority, his two doctoral degrees, my mother's talent. When they divorced, for many years thereafter I was unsure of myself. When it turned out that I could manage on my own in a foreign land, my juvenile anxieties passed, and I became self-confident.

"When I came here, I knew I had to follow the old principle, 'When in Rome, do as the Romans do'.

"I remember opening a series of lectures at the university with a joke . . . There were so many Polish jokes circulating then. 'Do you know who that is—a guy with a broken nose, missing two front teeth, and sporting a black eye?—That's the guy who told a Polish joke.'

"Students learned to pronounce my name correctly. They liked me and valued me as their teacher.

"In my opinion, I am a logical man. I often took my designs logically, thought them through. What do I owe my success to? . . . I worked hard, I used the maximum opportunities to achieve it.

"In America, a university professor does not enjoy the same prestige as they do in Europe. Here people say, 'Those who can—do, those who cannot—teach.'

"But I chose teaching consciously. Perhaps it is because I am European?

"I think that I know how to work hard, and that I have mental integrity. I owe a lot to my wife, who always helped me and offered advice. Our children have turned out well, they are honest, talented people. We wanted to give them a sense of roots, of origins. They know Polish traditions. We gave them rings with our family coat of arms, Leliwa.

" . . . I had an interesting life, but I would have preferred to work in Poland. Working for your country was a principle I was raised to believe in. But I have no regrets, I am liked and respected both by Poles and by Americans."

KRYSTYNA JAROSZEWICZ, NÉE BRZEZICKA

I also made notes of my conversations with Krystyna. She knew I was planning to write about her, as well. I sent her the text and she sent her corrections. It was similar with Marek, who also sent his corrections before I published my interview with him. She asked me not to publish anything about her then, maybe later. She considered the thoughts she'd shared with me too private, as if she were afraid to hurt someone with her words.

Now, years later, as I am writing their story, I would like to publish my notes from the conversations with her. I consider them important—true and very personal. And also full of pain which she seemed to be hiding inside her.

"The topics I am talking to you about, have been dormant for many years. I certainly do not talk or think of them every day. I would like to share my experiences, my thoughts, and you, Aleksandra, are willing to listen. It is strange: when I am in Poland and want to talk about the country I'm living in, everyone seems to know things better than me, about American politics or universities. Nobody asks me, everyone knows everything. *They* are lecturing *me* about America.

"I have a very tender attitude towards Poland, yet it is also painful. I share the sense of nationality with others. I am always sad to leave, and yet I am relieved. I am very tired mentally, with others' thoughts, their reactions to me, those incessant conversations which permeate to your core and cannot possibly be held daily. Life requires us to devote our time to various issues, not only analyzing, pondering, comparing . . . When I came to Poland for the first time in 1958, I cried so hard at the airport that the customs officer brought me some sedative. Each visit is an intense experience.

"When we came to the States, Marek and I said to ourselves: we are here, in this country, we must stand on our own two feet, no complaining, no lamenting, just work and achieve things. We applied for citizenship only after eight years.

"Life brought us to this particular shore, and we wanted to show the world and the people among whom we were living that we were interesting people. In Detroit, our American friends asked us, 'Are you related to Paderewski? . . . ' They knew nothing about the Polish intelligentsia back then, they were used to a different image of Poles. We wanted to prove that we were the same as the Americans, who thought the best of themselves; that were it not for the political situation in Poland, it would have been a prospering, attractive country. We were always sorry to see how many talents were bottled up in Poland.

"When people came from Poland, we helped them, to make it easier for them. There weren't many Poles here back then, we cared for their lives turning out well, because ' there would be more of us'. When Marek and I came here, we had nothing, not even a tea towel or a cup, we had to work for everything. Then we gave to others. Marek helped others find good jobs, he headed a committee which recognized architectural diplomas. He helped many people, not just Poles.

"What do I like Americans for? Why do I feel good here?..

"Americans like success and love optimism, they smile a lot. In America there is mutual friendliness, the principle is that 'the trough's large, there is enough for everyone' . . . They have such nice habits. When they come to visit, they always say they are glad to visit with us again, then call back to say thank you.

"When I was feeling ill and wore a warm scarf on my neck, the checkout assistant in the shop where I usually do shopping said, 'Are you all right?' On the next day she smiled and said, 'Oh, I see you're looking better!'

"When my sister Barbara visited us and went to the museum by herself, she told me later, 'Only now I believe what you say about America, now that I saw among the visitors a pregnant woman, an elderly lady with a walking stick, a young man in shorts, when I saw mothers with babies who left the baby carriages to see the pictures with their babies in their arms' . . .

"I am a practicing Catholic. I dare say that in America, the Catholics follow Church commandments more than those in my home country . . . But on the other hand, the churches in Poland are open all day long . . . I love visiting them . . . . Holy Cross Church with Saint Stanislaus altar, Jude the Apostle's (he answered my prayers once), St. Martin's Church, the Saviour's Church . . . I like going to confession in Poland.

"Social canons have changed in Poland. For instance, it is possible for one spouse to come to a meeting, while the other stays home with their chores. In the States it's unthinkable.

"In Poland, women are so emancipated and proud of it, but when I'm invited for a visit, the wife stays in the kitchen all the time, preparing the meal, and the husband entertains himself with the guests.

"I mind so many situations. When I came to Warsaw with my daughter, I heard that there was going to be a concert by Konstanty Kulka[21] in the Philharmonic. We really wanted to go and asked our friends where we could buy tickets. We were told to go to "Syrenka". I was there before 9 a.m., waiting for them to open. I was the fourth in the line. At 9:00 AM, they opened the door, we came in and formed the line again to wait. I heard, 'Władzia, would you have some sugar? . . . Oh, I broke my nail, do you have a file?'

"Finally she turned to the waiting people and started serving them. I asked if I could get tickets to Kulka's concert. 'We don't have any.'—'And tomorrow?' I asked.—'Please come tomorrow, we'll see.' I said that I really wanted to go, that I was there with my daughter, that the occasion would not arise again, because we lived in the States . . . 'Oh, so you have an American passport?' She gave me tickets, they had some after all. 'Am I someone better?' I asked. She didn't understand what I meant. Worse even, my friends didn't understand either. They often told me, 'Flash the passport and you'll get everything . . . ' They didn't understand it was humiliating for me.

"In Poland you fight for everything, in shops, in offices, it takes so much energy. I remember one scene from the Warsaw airport, as we were returning. The airport had no air conditioning, and the heat was unbearable. The customs officer came and asked, 'Which luggage is yours?' Stefan, my oldest son, jumped through some barrier and wanted to bring it. The officer ran up to him at once, caught his arm. 'You may not go here, leave it at once!' he snapped. I almost cried. My daughter Anna stroked my hand to calm me down. I didn't say anything, but she realized what state I was in. In Amsterdam, we changed planes. 'It was hot in Poland, would you like something to drink?' we were asked. 'Mommy, we are home,' my son said.

"In the Bristol Hotel in Warsaw, where I stayed with the kids, two very funny things happened. My son Jaś kept looking for some odd jobs. The old operator of the elevator kept saying to me, 'What a kind boy . . . ' It turned out that Jaś was helping him carry luggage, turned the crank to make the elevator work, and for the permission to do that he gave the old man cigarettes which he took from my suitcase. He knew his mom had a good supply of them.

"In front of the hotel, there was a woman selling water with raspberry juice from a cart. Jaś stood next to her and poured the juice, and later rinsed the glasses. She also said, 'What a kind boy . . . '

"When in Oliwa[22], I took the kids to an organ concert of Bach's works. They sat quiet like mice, lost in the music. Someone commented, 'For American kids, it is amazing that they listen to music quietly.'

"Or when I showed my kids' pictures, I heard, 'Your kids are so American, they grin so much . . . ' I started crying.

" . . . What do I love, what do I miss? . . . I miss Polish music, the Ujazdów Avenue, the beautiful royal Łazienki Park, memories, past experiences, incredible hospitality . . . When I get there, I know I am filling my roots with sap, that it has to last a long time. I like meeting old time friends. But I also avoid many topics.

"It hurts to hear from them, 'You just don't understand . . . '

"When I write to Poland, I put all of myself in the letters, release so many emotions. I sometimes didn't know how to write. When life was hard for me, I didn't want to share that. I thought, they had their own problems, life was so hard for them, there was that Stalinist Security Service. When I was better, or when I changed the house, I didn't know how to write about the event not to hurt anyone's feelings. Could I write, say, that we had a great holiday trip? . . . I thought, would it hurt them that I write of it so freely, while they could not leave anywhere?

"Our kids spoke Polish until they went to school. The youngest, Jaś, took the change the hardest. He got fevers daily, he suffered with his different, unpronounceable name. Those were the 1950s, the attitude towards foreign names was different than it is now. America was more provincial. The teacher asked me, 'Could he at least have a different first name? Or use his middle one—Mark?' It was actually Marek. Then I went then to the Mother Superior who ran a Catholic school, and she advised me to take him out of the public school. In the Catholic school, there was no problem with a foreign name or surname. I remember that when he played football, he was the hero of his team. The whole stand of spectators chanted, 'Jaś, Jaś!'—'See,' I pinched Marek's arm. 'They've learned!'

"The kids often said, 'Please, don't teach me Polish . . . ' My husband came back from work for dinner, and over the table there was the constant, 'Jaś, ask for the carrots in Polish, and you'll get them . . . '

"It was Marek's only contact with the kids, that dinner time. Different things were discussed, while there was always a strained atmosphere. Once he told me, 'I'd like to have some peace and quiet, I work 60 hours a week and I'd like a peaceful dinner.' Gradually, they started answering us in English when we spoke in Polish, and now we all speak English. Only if I am alone with Marek, Polish sounds again in our home. Once my kids used to call me '*Mamusieńka kochana, kochanie*' [Mommy dearest, love] . . . , and now more and more often it is just *Mom*.

"We gave it much thought, Marek and I, and we reached the conclusion that in Poland, you have kids all your life. All your life you have close contact with them, even daily. Often the housing conditions make people live together and even when kids become independent, they still count on their parents' help, and the parents do help out as much as they can. In America it is different. Children leave home rather early and become independent. But in America you also shape a sense of responsibility in the kids from a very young age. Adolescents work as babysitters, a sense of punctuality is developed, which does not seem to be observed in Poland.

" . . . There was much here in the States that irked us. We taught geography to our kids ourselves, the schooling level often left a lot to be desired. In a way, we supplemented their education, their knowledge.

"My children were born here and they are rooted here. This is their country. They don't have what I call the 'reopening inner wound'. For instance, English doesn't use words like 'soul/spirit' or 'honor' like the Polish do. And we were raised with a 'sense of 'honor'. English doesn't have that concept of the 'spirit', there is a concept of inner life, good or bad.

"We wanted to transfer to our children what is best in and about Poland. We also wanted to give them the same standard of life which we enjoyed before the war. (Marek's family had three maids for he and his father.) Our kids have no complexes. In Poland perhaps they would be burdened with a historical surname. I am glad they have grown into decent people. It may sound cruel, but I am glad they lost the Polish roots.

"What I often missed was family. Particularly when I had my children I felt the lack of mother or sister close by. I was jealous of those who had families with them.

"Marek and I are different. I am more interested in the person, what someone thinks, why thus and not different, I am interested in the inner life. Marek is interested in human experiences. We also read different books. He has a great mind. I always admire him because he could read something in, say, 'National Geographic' and two years later still be able to talk about what he'd read and remembered.

"We are also different in that he did not experience the Occupation. I react to many things in Poland differently. The Occupation made me so close to my country, took so much out of the beauty of life, and at the same time brought such great shocks.

"I remember Marek often saying, 'I'd give a lot to build a school in Poland, here I build things all the time. It's a pity it's not for the young people back home . . . '

"But the Polish issues slowly faded, and now Marek has more in common with any architect than with a Polish neighbor.

"After some harder time and years of hard work, we live an affluent, though not a rich life according to American standards. Studies for our four children cost us over 100 thousand dollars. Perhaps we will move to the south of Florida, as we have more Polish friends there. We won't be going back to the northern American climate.

"At my age, I think what I might have liked to do yet? . . . I would like to write memoirs for my grandchildren, so that they know why we are here and not there. I would like to gather now the crop of all those years of hardship, be among friends, read. I would like an easy old age, and also an easy, mild end . . . "

***

She asked me to meet her family when I came to Poland. And so in Warsaw, I visited Krystyna's sister, Barbara, and Marek's cousin Ewa.

Krystyna called me often. She preferred to talk of the situation in Poland rather than her health. She kept in regular touch with Zofia Korbońska. She rarely spoke about her kids. I knew their names: Stefan, Anna, Jan, Matthew. I met only the youngest son in their home.

She also wrote me short letters. Below I quote some fragments:

(15 VI 1992) I am very sorry to hear of your Father's passing. I went through that 38 years ago (my Father died in the Stalinist times—no telegrams, not to mention a visa to Poland—and I know how painful that is. In my case, I could not even pay the proverbial last respects to him. Please do not feel guilty—it was fate which had you live abroad. You have not renounced your family, it was simply the workings of fate. It is good that you visit your Mother, and it is so fortunate that there are no legal or financial problems with your visits to Poland.(. . .)

(27 VI 1995) Imagine that we finally bought a computer and my husband is extremely enthusiastic about becoming proficient with what is pretty much a toy for an American child . . .

(. . .) Oleńka[23], Christmas outside of Poland is always full of emotions, and that never changes . . . Please keep us au courant with Tomek's and your life.

(. . .) Dear Oleńka! How are you doing? I was in Poland for the 50 th anniversary of the Uprising and there was so much emotion, so many tears

and so much laughter (!) when meeting my friends from the Home Army. The Powązki Military Cemetery, 1ˢᵗ of August—that was my Poland!

I saw a mass of old friends and drew Polishness into my lungs and my heart.

(. . .) Dear Oleńka, Our Polish topics are so long and complex that I lack space for them in a Christmas card. I will contact you after Christmas because I would like to hear from you about your stay in Poland and in Paris.

(. . .) Dear Aleksandra, I was in Poland in July and froze to the bone— there was no summer weather. We are living quietly and taking care of each other. I have lots of time for reading and for music.

This year some health trouble caught up to us and preoccupied us completely. Our contacts with family and friends were limited to phone calls over letters, as both our mental and physical strength had been taxed.

We are glad for you when we hear of Tomek's good results and new publications. We hope the successes continue."

***

Marek Jaroszewicz died suddenly when he was visiting Warsaw with Krystyna on 23ʳᵈ July 1999. He was buried in his family tomb in Powązki.

Krystyna told me later that she considered that an act of Divine Providence that it happened in the city that was so dear to both of them.

The couple resigned themselves to the thought that they'd be buried in the American Częstochowa Cemetery in Doylestown.

On returning to the States, she sent me the speech the priest had given during the funeral mass for Marek Jaroszewicz in St. Borromeo's Church in Warsaw. There is a fragment with which I wholeheartedly agree:

"He was a charming man—he immediately established contact with the people he met. His comprehensive education and broad interests allowed him to immediately adjust to any environment. His conversational ability and fantastic sense of humor won people over to him, and contact with him was for his friends not only a pleasure, but also a valuable and unforgettable intellectual experience.

It is worth mentioning that among his many talents he was extremely musical. He said himself that if not for his greatest passion—architecture— he would have been a pianist.

Together with his great love since his schools days, and later his wife, Krystyna, they raised four children, giving them education and also the fundamentals of ethical and dignified life. They were a model family, with the best Polish tradition always cultivated.

Until the end of his life, Marek was closely attached to Poland, which fact he always stressed in his American environment. He was an ambassador for Polishness in the full sense of the word, aware of how limited the knowledge was about our country, its culture and its traditions.

His patriotism was not that of dramatic speeches, but that of effective, practical action. His help for people coming to the States in various periods of post-war immigration was invaluable. The Mareks' house, as they were always called, was a haven for the newcomers from Poland, lost in the foreign world, where they received help in taking their first steps in their careers. Thanks to his contacts they found jobs and could develop further.

He came often and gladly to Poland. Destiny had him see the end of that beautiful life during his last visit in his homeland."

Krystyna wrote to Norman in English:
(August 1999) *"Indeed Mark was an exceptional man—great brain, great heart and full of noble thoughts and deeds".*

***

After Marek's death, Krystyna Jaroszewicz moved to the south of Florida.

For the 60th anniversary of the Warsaw Uprising, several main channels of American TV showed David Ensor's[24] documentary about the Uprising, titled *CNN presents: Warsaw Rising*. It was repeated by many stations on the 60th anniversary of its outbreak. People speaking in the documentary included Zbigniew Brzeziński, Norman Davies[25], Zofia Korbońska and Krystyna Jaroszewicz.

In that last period she wrote less, but remained in regular phone contact.

The last two cards:

"Dear Aleksandra, I have problems with my eyes and it's difficult to write so just a short message . . . "(. . .)

"Dear Oleńka, It's so hard for me to get used to being alone, but I don't give up."

She died on the 29th September 2006. In the next year, her ashes were brought to the Warsaw Powązki cemetery to rest next to her husband.

Both are now resting in their beloved city—Warsaw.

***

In Gulbiny, where they'd first met, the remains of the wooden manor stood until 1959. Today there is no trace of it anymore, but there are still fragments of the park with old linden trees, oaks, hornbeams and maples, and the linden avenue still leads you from where the manor once stood towards the village.

NOTES

1. Zofia Korbońska, née Ristau (born 1915 in Warsaw, died 2010 in Washington, D.C.) was a Polish resistance fighter and journalist.

2. Aleksandra Ziółkowska-Boehm, "Amerykanie z wyboru," Warsaw 1998, pp. 50-69, Aleksandra Ziółkowska-Boehm, "The Roots Are Polish," Toronto 1999, pp. 131-147; inter-

view with Marek Jaroszewicz "Nie lubie szuflad dla ludzi..." (I do not like pigeonholes for people...) in "Przeglad Powszechny", No. 5 1995, pp. 170-179.

3. In 1922 Marian Piwnicki's daughter Helena married Bolesław Brzezicki, of the Topór coat of arms. The Brzezickis turned out to be the last owners of the estate up to the outbreak of WWII in 1939. Both were killed in their manor by the Germans.

4. Fryderyk Franciszek Chopin (1810-1849), famous Polish composer and a virtuoso pianist. He gained and has maintained renown worldwide as one of the leading musicians of his era, Chopin was born near and grew up in Warsaw. A child prodigy, he completed his musical education and composed his earlier works in Warsaw before leaving Poland at the age of 20, less than a month before the outbreak of the November 1830 Uprising. He died in Paris. Chopin requested that his body be opened after death (for fear of being buried alive) and his heart returned to Warsaw where it rests at the Church of the Holy Cross.

5. See: Zofia Jeżewska, "Chopin w kraju rodzinnym" (Chopin in His Home Country), Wyd. PTTK "Kraj", Warsaw 1985.

6. Maria Rodziewiczówna (1863-1944)—Polish writer among the most famous of the interwar years. The outbreak of WWII found her in Hruszowa. When the Russians encroached, she was displaced in October 1939, and the estate was seized.

7. Melchior Wańkowicz (1892–1974) a Polish popular writer. He is most famous for his reporting of the Polish Armed Forces in the Westduring World War II and writing a book about the battle of Monte Cassino. See: Aleksandra Ziolkowska-Boehm, Melchior Wańkowicz: Poland's Master of the Written Word, Lexington Books, Lanham, MD 2013.

8. Czesław Miłosz (1911–2004) a Polish poet, prose writer, translator. Following the war, he served as Polish cultural attaché in Paris and Washington, D.C., then in 1951 defected to the West. From 1961 to 1998 he was a professor of Slavic Languages and Literatures at the University of California, Berkeley. In 1978 he was awarded the Neustadt International Prize for Literature, and in 1980 the Nobel Prize in Literature. He died in Krakow, Poland.

9. The Government Delegation for Poland was an agency of the Polish Government in Exile during World War II, and the highest authority of the Polish Secret State in occupied Poland. The Government Delegate for Poland acted as deputy Polish Prime Minister. The Government Delegation for Poland was intended as a provisional government of Poland until the Exiled Polish Government could safely return once the country was liberated.

10. Maria countess Tarnowska, of the Sviatopolk-Chetvertynsky princely family (1880-1965), daughter of Włodzimierz Sviatopolk-Chetvertynsky, veteran of the 1863 January Uprising, and Maria Wanda of the Uruski counts. Wife to count Adam Tarnowski. During WWI she worked as a nurse, and during the 1920 Polish-Soviet War as the commandant of a Red Cross unit. After the war, she was a board member of the Polish Red Cross. During WWII she was arrested in 1942 and spent several months in the Pawiak prison. On release, she joined the underground forces and received the rank of a lieutenant of the Home Army, then a major in September 1944. Due to her high social rank and experience she was delegated to talks with the Germans concerning the evacuation of civilians, which enabled 20-25 thousand people, mainly women, children and the elderly, to leave Warsaw on 8th-10th September 1944. She participated also in the capitulation negotiations. Arrested in 1945 by the communist Citizens' Militia on charges of collaborating with the Germans, she was held for a month in Olkusz. She stayed abroad in 1946-1958, then returned to Poland. She died in Warsaw.

11. Gestapo seat and prison.

12. Melchior Wańkowicz, "Ziele na kraterze" (Herbs at the Crater), Warsaw 1971, p. 389.

13. Archiwum Historii Mówionej (Spoken History Archive), Warsaw Uprising Museum http://ahm.1944.pl/Tadeusz%20_Olszewski.

14. Polska Organizacja Wojskowa (POW)—secret military organization created by Józef Piłsudski in 1914, during World War I, to gather intelligence and sabotage the enemies of the Polish people.

15. 1920 Kiev Offensive or Kiev Operation—a military operation of the armed forces of Poland led by Józef Piłsudski in alliance with the Ukrainian leader Symon Petliura, which was an attempt to seize the territories of modern-day Ukraine which fell under the Soviet control after the Bolshevik Revolution, and to create a formally independent Ukraine. The operation led to a Soviet counteroffensive, and ended amicably with the formal Peace of Riga of 1921.

16. Ignacy Jan Paderewski (1860–1941) a Polish pianist and composer, politician, and spokesman for Polish independence. He was a favorite of concert audiences around the globe. His musical fame opened access to diplomacy and the media. He played an important role in meeting with President Woodrow Wilson and obtaining the explicit inclusion of independent Poland. He was the Prime Minister of Poland and also Poland's foreign minister in 1919, and represented Poland at the Paris Peace Conference in 1919. He served ten months as Prime Minister. He died in New York and was buried in Arlington National Cemetery, in Arlington,Virginia, near Washington, D.C. In 1992, his body was brought to Warsaw and placed in St. John's Arch cathedral.

17. Eero Saarinen (1910–1961)—Finnish American architect, one of the greatest American architects of the 20th century. His more important projects include e.g. the General Motors Technical Center in Detroit, the Massachusetts Institute of Technology in Cambridge, the TWA Flight Center at J.F.K. International Airport and the main terminal of the Dulles International Airport near Washington, D.C.

18. Zbigniew Brzezinski (born 1928 in Warsaw, Poland)—Polish-American political scientist and geostrategist, counsellor to President Lyndon B. Johnson (1966-68), President Jimmy Carter's National Security Advisor (1977-81). Author.

19. Józef Lipski (1894—1958) was a Polish diplomat and Ambassador to Nazi Germany (1934 to 1939). Lipski played a key role in the foreign policy of the Second Polish Republic.

During the Second World War, Lipski fought as a volunteer (Polish 1st Grenadiers Division in France) and later joined the General Staff of the Polish Armed Forces in the West. In 1951 Lipski moved to the USA and represented the Polish Government in Exile.

20. Thaddeus Michael Machrowicz (1899–1970) was a politician and judge from the U.S. state of Michigan. He was born in Gostyń, Poland and immigrated to the United States with his parents in 1902.

21. Konstanty Andrzej Kulka (born 1947)—Polish violinist, recording artist, and professor of the Fryderyk Chopin University of Music in Warsaw. He played over 1,500 recitals internationally, including in the United States, Japan, and Australia, and is a guest performer with the Berliner Philharmoniker, Chicago Symphony Orchestra, London Symphony Orchestra, English Chamber Orchestra, Royal Concertgebouw Orchestra in Amsterdam, Minneapolis Symphony Orchestra, and Saint Petersburg Philharmonic Orchestra.

22. A district of Gdańsk, Poland. The Oliwa cathedral has two organs: a small choir organ from 2003 with a 16th century case, and the big main organ built 1763 - 1788. The organ case is unique in the world and is considered one of the largest cases worldwide. There is a twenty-minute organ concerto organized daily in the cathedral, beside larger, scheduled concerts.

23. Oleńka—Polish nick name for Aleksandra.

24. David Ensor, journalist for National Public Radio, ABC News, and CNN. 28th Director of the Voice of America. Previously he was Director for Communications and Public Diplomacy of the U.S. Embassy in Kabul, Afghanistan.

25. Norman Richard Davies (born 1939 in Bolton, Lancashire)—British-Polish historian noted for his publications on the history of Europe, Poland and the United Kingdom, widely regarded as one of the preeminent historians of Central and Eastern European history. UNESCO Professor at the Jagiellonian University, Professor Emeritus at the University College London, a Visiting Professor at the College of Europe and an Honorary Fellow at St. Antony's College, Oxford.

Tadeusz Brzezinski. Archives of and used by permission of Zbigniew Brzezinski.

Zbigniew Brzezinski. Archives of and used by permission of Zbigniew Brzezin-ski.

Zbigniew Brzezinski with his daughter Mika, wife Emilie (née: Benes). Virginia 1989. Archives of and used by permission of Zbigniew Brzezinski.

Zbigniew Brzezinski, N.N., Aleksandra Ziolkowska-Boehm, Warsaw 1994. Archives of Aleksandra Ziolkowska-Boehm.

February 3, 1998

Dear Ms Ziolkowska-Boehm:

Thank you for your recent note. I am writing separately to the PEN Club, recommending strongly your admission. You are a natural as a member!

With warm personal regards,

Sincerely,

Zbigniew Brzezinski

Ms Aleksandra Ziolkowska-Boehm
13 Servan Court. Parkway West
Wilmington, DE 19805

O Hubalczyku czytałam jednym tchem!

1800 K Street Northwest • Washington DC 20006 • Telephone 202/887-0200
FAX: 202/775-3199

Dedication and Letters. Archives of Aleksandra Ziolkowska-Boehm.

CSIS

Center for Strategic & International Studies
Washington, DC

June 20, 2001

Dear Aleksandra:

Many thanks for your letter of June 14 and the enclosed two books. You are most productive, and the two volumes – into which I have started dipping – are quite impressive.

Thanks also for your general update. I was struck by your reference to the Crazy Horse sculpture. I did not know that this was being done by your uncle. You may be interested to know that Trudy has just been there and was most impressed by it.

As to dogs: we are, indeed, a dog-owning family, but, frankly, I have too much on my plate right now to write about them. When I am finished with the Chinese and the Russians, perhaps someday I will have time to deal with the dogs!

With best regards,

Cordially,

Zbigniew Brzezinski

Ms Aleksandra Ziolkowska-Boehm
11 Ridgewood Circle
Wilmington, DE 19809

Dedication and Letters. Archives of Aleksandra Ziolkowska-Boehm.

For Aleksandra Ziółkowska-
Boehm

with admiration for
her creativity!

Dedication and Letters. Archives of Aleksandra Ziolkowska-Boehm.

September 5, 2014

Dear Aleksandra,

Thank you so much for sending me the very impressive volume regarding not only Monte Cassino but also other aspects of the enduring Polish struggle for independence and democracy. It will be occupying an important place in my library.

Best regards,

Zbigniew Brzezinski

Aleksandra Ziolkowska-Boehm
11 Ridgewood Circle
Wilmington, DE 19809

Dedication and Letters. Archives of Aleksandra Ziolkowska-Boehm.

Rudolf S. Falkowski, Air Force Officer Training Centre, Stanisławów, April 1939.
Photo from the archives of and used by permission of Stefan Władysiuk.

Wiesław Chrzanowski. Photo from the archives of and used by permission of
Marta Chrzanowska-Ławniczak.

Halina Chrzanowska. Photo from the archives of and used by permission of
Marta Chrzanowska-Ławniczak.

Warsaw Rising 1944. Photo by Wieslaw Chrzanowski - from the archives of and used by permission of Marta Chrzanowska-Ławniczak.

Marek Jaroszewicz. Archives of Aleksandra Ziolkowska-Boehm.

Maria Kowal, 1950. I.D. Issued at the Resettlement Processing Center in Wentorf before coming to the United States. Photo from the archives of and used by permission of Mary and Tony Kowal.

Maria Kowal and Monarch Butterfly. Mary and her son Tony raise Monarch and Swallowtail Butterflies. The Swallowtail beauties are shiny black in color with a border of rich sapphire blue or yellow border. In the summer of 2016 they raised 128 Monarchs and 4 Swallowtails. Photo from the archives of and used by permission of Mary and Tony Kowal.

Maria Kowal - The stairs in St. Peter & Paul Cathedral in Łuck (now: Lutsk), where she was born (on June 5, 1943). 70 years later - June 5th, 2013. Photo from the archives of and used by permission of Mary and Tony Kowal.

Janina i Stanisław Batorski, Lwow, 1932. Photo from the archives of and used by permission of Danuta Batorska.

From left: Ina and Marion Andre, Aleksandra Ziolkowska-Boehm. Toronto 1987 at apartment of Janusz Dukszta. Photo by Thomas Tomczyk. Used by permission of Thomas Tomczyk.

only by courage of this order that Colombia will ~~that recognize~~ ~~both the federal gov~~
loosen the evil grip that threatens its survival as a situation and the need to replace the old tax. A
decent country. *Globe and Mail, 25 Sept. 1989, Toronto* Wilson and his cabinet colleagues listening?

LETTERS T

X Life saved by Poles

I am a Jew and a survivor of the Holocaust. I am compelled to contradict Israeli Prime Minister Yitzhak Shamir, who, as you reported Sept. 9, apparently stated in an interview that Poles are anti-Semitic from birth, that "they suck it with their mother's milk. This is something that is deeply imbued in their tradition, their mentality" (Poles Born Anti-Semitic, Shamir Says).

I need to say with passion that I am alive today because of the help of several Polish Christians.

During the German occupation of Poland, I escaped from the ghetto in the city of Lvov. I was assisted by a Polish Christian man who supplied me with forged documents and a Polish Christian woman who helped me reach Warsaw by accompanying me on the train. I lived in Warsaw with three Polish Christian families who were aware of my origin and were proud to have me in their homes in spite of the fact that a verdict of death might be their fate, because such was the Nazi policy for those who concealed Jews.

The woman who helped me become a "free" man also saved my mother. She helped her cross the barbed-wire fence border of the Lvov ghetto and brought her by train to Warsaw, where she arranged for her to stay in the home of a Polish Christian family. My mother was treated with loving care by those people of low income, and lived there in hiding until the collapse of the Warsaw uprising in 1944. Then she and the family were moved by the Germans to a small town where she survived the war and came to live in Canada.

Was there anti-Semitism in Poland? Yes. Many Poles despised the Jews. I witnessed and suffered occasionally from their prejudice as a teenager. I am certain such people still exist there as they exist in other countries. But to say that the whole Polish nation was/is like that is false.

Not all Poles were/are Jew haters. Therefore I rebel against such a preposterous generality as the one expressed by Mr. Shamir. That

is the reason for this letter. To fulfil my need to speak in defence of the Polish Christians who risked their lives to save Jews.

What I have said should not be interpreted as a concession to those who believe the Carmelite convent should remain on the site of Auschwitz concentration camp (the Vatican said it should be moved). That place should be left intact as a memorial to Jewish martyrdom. And as a gruesome reminder to what level human cruelty can soar when the counterforce — the sense of brotherhood, love and justice — stays silent.

Marion Andre
Founding Artistic Director
of Theatre Plus
Toronto

Sold-out trains

I find it difficult to believe the federal government is considering reducing passenger services in the Maritimes and claiming lack of use of these services as its excuse. When attempting to travel midweek at a non-peak period to Ottawa, I was unable to get a seat because both trains were sold out.

Imagine my surprise when the station attendant informed me that my experience was not unique and that these trains are sold out more often than not.

On the return trip, I purchased my ticket well ahead of time and the train was once again filled up. Perhaps the federal government should re-examine the real passenger levels before cutting back this important service.

Tim Baycroft
Sackville, N.B.

Minor changes expected

In your Sept. 8 editorial, The Shifting Ground In South Africa, you said, "the white tribe of South Africa no longer speaks with a single voice." It never has, as there are two white tribes, the majority Afrikaners, formerly known as Boers, and the English speakers, largely of British descent.

"The breakdown of consensus in the white tribe," you said, "must mean the breakdown of apart-

Scurrying to safety as the N

Exhibit o

The fire on board the S.S. N Sept. 16 (The Fiery Death Of indeed a tragic chapter in the which brings back many pain years ago, the Marine Museu exhibit on the fire, which is sti tion Place.

As part of the exhibit's ope their memories of that night, part of the museum's collectio

In addition to the ship's de heard at the museum, the To contains a life-ring, the ship's of the bow flagstaff with the b there exists more of the ship th

R. Scott James
Managing Director
Toronto Historical Board

heid." Would that it was so. Unf tunately, it was largely the En lish-speaking electors who vo for the Democratic Party, whic committed to real change, wh the vast majority of the Afrikan voted for the Nationalists or

A golden opportunity to n

"Globe and Mail", Toronto 25, 1989.

Tomasz Lychowski and his mother Gertruda, Warsaw 1938. Photo from the archives of and used by permission of Tadeusz Lychowski.

Tomasz Lychowski and his father, after the war, 1946. Photo from the archives of and used by permission of Tadeusz Lychowski.

Warsaw Ruins. Old City Market Square, bombed by Germans after Rising 1944. Photo by Jan Bulhak - from the archives of and used by permission of Bohdan Bulhak.

Warsaw Ruins. Old City 1945. Photo by Jan Bulhak - from the archives of and used by permission of Bohdan Bulhak.

Chapter Five

"I was that child about to be born..."

Maria Kowal

I was told about Maria Kowal from Chicago by Wiesław Adamczyk, author of the book "Kiedy Bóg odwrócił wzrok"(*When God Looked the Other Way*).

"Call her and listen to her story . . . Just how many people are born in a cathedral? . . . and the Soviets, the Germans . . . She will be waiting for your call."

Our conversations grew longer, more frequent, almost daily, and reached even beyond the memories of Maria, called Marysia by Wiesław, and Mary in the States. We did not talk about America, and not of what she stored in her memory, but of events which she heard about so many times that they are rooted deeply in her mind, almost as if she had seen and remembered them herself . . . Yet seen them she could not have, for she was then a seven-month-old fetus in her mother's womb . . .

The events she told me about, I recall here as they were told, in the first person. Using the form of monologue, I find it possible not only to bring back the events, but to better present my particular amazement, that people could have suffered such turns of fate . . . And those people were her dearest family.

. . . What I am telling you now, was told to me many times by my Mom, Dad, and my older siblings, so it feels as if I'd been there with them.

So many years have passed, and the older I am, the more I think of my parents—think of them with a kind of painful understanding.

My family lived in the Pendyki village in Volhynia. My parents lived in one house, and the grandparents, the aunts: Hela, Zosia and Kasia and their families in other houses. Pendyki was largely inhabited by Poles, with only one Ukrainian family. My maternal grandparents Marianna and Franciszek

Bąk, came from a village of Trembowiec near Radom. Grandfather was a forester there. In 1927 they left to Volhynia to find a better life for themselves and their family. They took their children with them, among them the deaf-mute Władysława, as well as Zofia (Zosia). Katarzyna (Kasia), Helena (Hela), Stanisław, and my Mom Waleria, the oldest of the siblings were already married. Waleria and her husband Józef Sieczka used to live in another village, Zbijów Duży, with their children Władzio and Helenka. In Pendyki, the family increased with Janek, Ludwik, Antoś, and they were expecting another child.

In Pendyki, my grandparents, parents and aunts had their own little farms, which brought joy and money. In the early morning of 25th March 1943[1], my then 15-year-old brother Janek (Johnny, as I called him here) heard screams of people and nervous bellows of animals. He looked out through the door and saw a huge fire—as if the whole village was burning. He awakened the family—everyone started to run without hesitation.

During that Spring it was still cold in the mornings. My father wanted to harness a horse to their cart, and he wanted to put an eiderdown in it for my pregnant Mom, but the horse shied and ran away. My Mom was 7 months pregnant. I was that child about to be born.

Holding the hands of the 9-year-old Antoś (Tony) and 13-year-old Ludwik (Louie), Mom first wanted to hide in the potato cellar behind the house. Yet Ludwik pulled at her as strongly as he could, trying to convince her not to stop, because the fire was too close to the house already. Years later, my parents told me that people and animals were running any which way, people trying to escape gunshots. Bullets were flying in the air. Fire was not the only threat—the Ukrainians shot at the running Poles, others had axes, knives and pitchforks, with which they struck at people. My parents told me later that those had been Ukrainian nationalists, OUN-UPA units.[2]

My parents also learned later that the only Ukrainian family in Pendyki helped a Polish family by hiding them.

On escaping, my parents didn't know what had happened to the rest of the family, the grandparents and the aunts.

My sister Helena, nearly 20 then, ran first to a friend and only later joined the family. Chaos, terror, fear and dread all reigned. Everyone ran through the woods to the nearby town of Tsuman.

. . . I can hardly imagine, Aleksandra, what they must have been going through.

As the whole family walked on, near Tsuman, they encountered some German soldiers driving by. When the soldiers saw my pregnant Mom, they took Mom and the kids, along with others in the truck and brought them to a church.[3]

There was already a large group of Poles there, from Pendyki and nearby Deraźne. There was also Aunt Kasia. They learned she had left the house (where her sister-in-law Stefania stayed with four of her children) holding her two-year-old son Mieciuś by the hand, the other arm holding a pillow cradling six months old daughter Zosia. One of the bandits pushed her and threw the pillow with Zosia to the ground, asking, "Where's your husband?" "Oh, they'd already got him, he'd dead," she lied. "And the kids are whose?" "I just found them around," she said half-joking, not knowing why she answered thus, as if defensive in her deep fear. The Ukrainian man took a closer look and yelled, "Get those kids and leave here at once, I don't want to see you … " She picked Zosia up and ran. She made it to Tsuman, where her husband, my Uncle Wacław was already waiting for her.[4]

Everyone wore the same clothing they had been wearing since that early morning. The local Poles brought some food. Nobody knew anything, and everyone worried about those who had been left behind.

Two days later my father, Uncle Wacław—Aunt Kasia's husband—and one more man decided to go and see what had happened with Pendyki. I don't know if they went on foot or if someone gave them a lift.

It turned out that our house was partly burned and utterly ransacked; furniture, bedlinen, literally everything had been taken or destroyed. Father picked up a few pictures and documents from the floor, and a picture of St Anthony, once framed by my grandfather. The picture survived and is now hanging in my bedroom.

They went from one house to the other. Most houses were partly burned, like ours. Around there lay bodies and, as they learned later, about 150 people were murdered.

Eleven of them were members of our family. My grandma and two Aunts, Marianna and Władysława, had been beaten with a metal rod from the fence, which lay beside them. Another Aunt, Stefania, and her four children had been suffocated in their home. My Uncle Mietek and grandpa had been shot.

Here, I name everyone:

Grandmother Marianna Bąk, 71; Aunt Władysława Bąk, 30; Aunt Marynia (Marianna) Bąk (mother of Uncle Mietek, who'd been shot); grandfather Franciszek, 72, asthmatic, he could not catch his breath, sat down and a bullet found him; Aunt Stefania Bąk and her four children—Kazia, Jadzia, Wandzia and Marian—suffocated by stopping the chimney with straw which was then set on fire. Together with our "adoptive" Aunt, Józia and her little son had died—she had been friends with Aunt Stefania and the children. Uncle Mietek, married to Jadwiga Bąk, was shot with a pistol bullet.

His wife—my Mom's sister—escaped to Tsuman.

. . . You're asking about the book "The Genocide Committed by Ukrainian Nationalists on the Polish Population of Volhynia 1939-1945."[5]

Siemaszkos's book wrongly states that Mom's brother, Stanisław Bąk, the husband of Aunt Stefania—the one killed with four children—had also been killed. Uncle Stanisław hid somewhere and managed to get to Łuck.

There he saw a Ukrainian man wearing his father's boots. Uncle knew them, because he'd made them himself . . . Uncle Stanisław beat that Ukrainian severely and later had to stay in hiding because he was wanted. None of us knew what had happened to him. Later, in the States, Mom found him through numerous letters to various institutions. She learned that he was living in Russia with a new family. They started writing to each other. She sent him 100 dollars for his daughter's wedding, but she never received a confirmation, or another letter. She didn't know what happened to him.

Father, Uncle Wacław and that one accompanying man couldn't even bury the dead in Pendyki, as it was too dangerous. They returned to the families they'd left in the church.

After a few days the people hiding in Tsuman were told it was dangerous to stay there any longer. When the parish priest, Fr. Stefan Zawadzki, left the church, he was attacked by Ukrainians, who slit his throat and threw him into a ditch. People saved him, and he survived, but he lost his voice forever and moved with difficulty, forever disabled.[6]

The trek started again. Everyone wanted to get from Tsuman to Łuck (now: Lutsk), located some 47 kilometers (30 miles) away. It was a long way. Mom and Dad reminisced after the years how terribly exhausted they had been. Antoś and Ludwik were very much weakened by the exhaustion and hunger. Antoś had blood on his lips and kept asking, "When do we get something to eat?" "Soon, son, soon we'll be in Łuck and God will give us food," answered Mom.

I don't know how it might have ended, they were growing weaker by the day . . . Later my sister and my Mom said they'd met an angel on their way . . . thus they called a good woman who on seeing the family shared her bread. She had two loaves and gave one to Mom. They didn't know anything about her, and she saved them from hunger. "See, baby, God gave us bread," said Mom to Antoś.

I remember that years later Mom would talk about the woman, for whom she prayed until her death.

Like others, our family stayed in the Łuck cathedral. It was a historic building from the early 17th century, Peter and Paul the Apostles's Cathedral.

. . . And I was born there, on 5th June 1943. Aunt Zosia, Mom's sister, gave a shawl in which to wrap me up after birth.

Five weeks later everyone was taken in a freight train to Germany. The camp was in Kiel.

My parents worked from six in the morning to six in the evening. Before leaving the barrack in the morning, they only had some black bread with chicory coffee. Mom saved a portion of the bread for later. On returning in the evening, they received a bowl of watered soup, made from turnips. At times, they would find insects floating in the soup. Along with a piece of bread and coffee that was their day's nutrition. Mom and others had to dig graves for German soldiers killed in bombings by the Allied forces.

In the nearby town of Reisdorf, my father loaded various wares on train cars, and Janek worked there in a coal mine. Hela worked first with father, and then in a warehouse. The Soviets took Władek to a Russian camp, and later, he said they'd beaten him very badly, along with starving him and the other inmates.

My brother Ludwik somehow became friends with a German woman working in a German kitchen. Knowing there was an infant in the family, she gave him food. She was a good woman, as she was putting herself at risk. Sometimes my father repaired the boots of German soldiers, and brought something more to eat, too.

I was protected from "bombi" (that's how children called bombs) by being placed in fox holes dug by the children. After work, Mom found me dirty, wet, and screaming with hunger.

. . . I cannot even imagine all that . . . I'm just repeating to you what I've been told by my parents throughout the years . . . We all survived by the grace of God.

When the war ended in 1945, we were again sent from camp to camp, but there was no working anymore. We were all brought to the German island Sylt in the North Sea. I was growing up and remember a little from that time. For instance, in Lübeck father bought me a banana for my sixth birthday, and I didn't know what to do with it until I was shown.

My brothers Ludwik and Antoni went to school in the German town of Pinneburg near Hamburg. Ludwik was very gifted and was included in a group under a program sponsored by the Polish American Congress. He left to Junction City, Wisconsin, near Stevens Point, to continue his education. A farmer, Frank Kowalski, agreed to sponsor the rest of the family. He was of Polish origin and had a farm in Edgar, Wisconsin.

And so in the winter of 1950 we came to the States. Father was 58, Mom was 48, Antoś was 15, and I was 6.

We went by ship to Boston, from there by train to Union Station in Chicago, and further to Wisconsin. My brother waited for us in the station with a bag of oranges, which were completely unknown to me then.

My parents helped our sponsor around the farm. After six months, were able to move to Chicago, where Ludwik was attending school. To this day, I still have contact with Frank Kowalski's family.

My siblings: brothers Janek and Władzio and sister Helenka, were still in a German camp in Meierwik/Glücksburg. My sister got married there in 1946 and had two children. She came to the States two years after we did. Later, Janek and Władzio also came. After three years, we were together again.

I remember that the Poles who had come and settled there well before the war laughed at the newcomers and called us DP [displaced persons-AZB], which hurt. My parents managed—Father worked in a factory producing boxes, and Mom worked with holiday cards in Century Engraving.

Thus started our life in the United States.

In Wisconsin, I started going to school, and I started it again in Chicago, because I still knew no English. I soon became a good student, both in primary school and in high school. I wanted to be a nurse and passed the entrance exams to Loyola University, but my parents didn't have the money to pay for my education. I worked in an office as a receptionist and attended evening college classes, learning accountancy. I liked accounting, and with it my career began.

When I was nearing 25, in 1968, I married Robert Kowal. His mother came to the USA from Poland after WWI, when she was 16. He was my elder by 19 years, born in 1925, now a tax advisor and accountant. Robert was very attached to the Polish tradition, language and history and that was another thing we had very much in common. I suffered two miscarriages. Our only son Tony was named after my brother, Antoni. Tony has obtained a Ph.D. in molecular biology at Northwestern University.

My husband died in 2009, after our 40th wedding anniversary. I took care of him those last few years, as he had vascular dementia.

In June 2013, I went with my son to Łuck, Ukraine. I wanted to see it for my 70th birthday, to see where I was born. We went to the cathedral which I remembered from the stories told by my parents and older siblings. They told me I'd been born in a room behind the choir. My son and I went up there, climbing the steep, railing-less stairs. It was difficult to climb up there . . . "How did Mom get up there being seven months pregnant?" I wondered.

We talked in Polish with a Ukrainian nun named Sister Oksana. She said she'd heard that during the war people had sought shelter in the cathedral and the church buildings.

. . . Now that I looked back, I realize that I've always seen the strength of my parents. They suffered through so much pain and injustice, but they never broke, never lost their faith. They are to a large extent responsible for the faith I have and my not giving up characteristic. They have been always the source of strength and spirit to me.

My Mom seemed a cold woman at first glance, didn't kiss us kids or hug us. Now I think of her with great respect and love, and understand her so well. She must have been like that to survive.

I can't remember Mom or Dad ever trying to rationalize UPA crimes. And I must admit that on seeing a modern-day Ukrainian I cannot stop remembering what had occurred. They'd stolen from me the joy of having grandparents, aunts and uncles. They'd stolen my childhood. My parents were very brave, but they never quite recovered from the tragedy the family suffered.

My father died in 1989 at the age of 96. Mom was 90 when she died in 1992. I was there with both of them when they died, and it is so important for me that I took care of them. In the same way I cared for and later buried my older brothers, and I'm caring for my 90-year-old sister Helena now.

What do I do now?...

... I do voluntary work at school, and raise Monarch butterflies.

Butterflies are my passion and my relaxation. I have various incubator boxes around the house, where I help them go through all stages of incubation. I like it when they dry their wings, waiting calmly for three or four hours. And then they start to move. I am so happy when they sit on my finger. Once, a butterfly sat on my son's finger for an hour and a half. Finally I set them free in the garden and it is like a holiday to me—a new life. Some Monarchs live a year. But as they fly, I am always happy.

At home I have paintings and many trinkets with a butterfly motif. They represent such a multicolor, quiet world.

NOTES

1. Some sources give 29th March, but this is what Mrs. Kowal's parents and siblings remembered.

2. OUN-UPA—the Organization of Ukrainian Nationalists and the Ukrainian Insurgent Army. The political leadership of the Ukrainian nationalist partisan army (UPA) belonged to the Organization of Ukrainian Nationalists—Bandera faction (OUN-B). It was created in 1942. It was mainly active in Volhynia and Eastern Galicia and west of the Curzon Line. Its aim was to create an independent, ethnically clean Ukrainian state. The Ukrainian Insurgent Army and the Organization of Ukrainian Nationalists share the responsibility for organising and conducting the genocide of Polish civilians (the Volhynia massacre and ethnic cleansing in Eastern Galicia). Estimates of the number of Poles killed by the UPA range from 60,000 to 100,000.

3. It was a St Augustin's parish church, built in 1936 by Duke Janusz Radziwiłł, after 1945 devastation and restructuring. It currently holds a cinema, and since 1994 Catholic services are held in the side aisle. The current administrator is Fr. Jerzy Nagórny.

4. They survived the war, and returned to Poland to settle in the village of Horyszów. Years later, her grown-up daughter Zosia visited their family in Chicago.

5. E. Siemaszko, W. Siemaszko, "Ludobójstwo dokonane przez nacjonalistów ukraińskich na ludności polskiej Wołynia 1939-1945," vol. I, Warsaw, von borowiecky, 2000.

6. He was the last parish priest of the church in Tsuman. He died in 1969.

Chapter Six

The Child from
Bialowieza Primeval Forest,
the Urals, Isfahan and Mexico

Danuta Batorska

Danuta Batorska is one of the rescued children who shared the fate of their parents, deported to the Urals, to Siberia, and then exited Russia with the Polish Army through Tehran and Isfahan. With her sister Krystyna Barbara (called Basia) and mother Janina (her father Stanisław Batorski remained in prison in the Urals), the two were brought from Isfahan to Mexico, where they stayed in the Santa Rosa settlement for Polish refugees. The sisters went to school in the settlement.

I met Janina and Danuta, mother and daughter, in Houston. I liked Texas and I felt good there. My husband Norman was preparing contract documents for Exxon. We spent eight years—with breaks—in Texas. My historic interests, fascination with the fates of Polish people, gave me repeatedly the painful satisfaction of meeting yet another person whose anticipated normal life was stolen away by World War II—they lost their homes, they lost their families.

Danuta Batorska was born in Hajnówka four years before the war broke out. Her father, Stanisław Batorski, a graduate of the Lviv Polytechnic Institute with a Master's degree in forestry, worked as a forest administrator in the Nikor inspectorate in the Białowieża Forest[1] beginning in 1935. Her mother, Janina Wiktoria Batorska nee Kucharska, was born in Lviv in 1908. The family Stanislaw, Janina and their children lived together in the Białowieża Forest. Nearby, Danuta's godfather also lived in the Forest; he too was a forest administrator, and as a hobby bred Arabian horses.

Danuta spent the first four years of her life surrounded by woods. Her memory unfailingly retains the natural beauty of the Białowieża Forest, the animals and the family's beloved dogs. She remembers the hunting parties. Guests would come, mother would cook a traditional *bigos*, and little Danusia (diminutive of Danuta) would scramble into the male guests' laps asking them to "draw her an uhlan[2]." She remembers as a little girl her adoration for the farmhand Stanisław. A vivid memory for Danuta was the Christmas tree at home in the winter . . .

She told me all the images left in her memory from that period are exceptional and are so much more moving as they are lost forever, cut off so suddenly and so early in her life.

Danuta remembers well the 1st of September 1939, the outbreak of the war, and the German planes descending to bomb people and cattle. Later, she always feared planes—she would try to escape them as she heard them come.

The Nikor forest inspectorate was on the very border with Belarus, and Danuta remembers Belarusians as very aggressive, anti Polish. On one occasion, they nearly killed her father. On 17th September, about two weeks after the German attack, Soviets crossed the eastern border into Poland.

Her father was captured and first put in prison in Białowieża, then released, and subsequently with the whole family was initially imprisoned to Druskininki, today in Lithuania. Her maternal grandmother from Lviv, Maria Kucharska, was deported with them, (her grandfather was killed in WWI). What was important, in Druskininki was the fact that the whole family was together.

On February 10, 1940 at five a.m., the NKVD[3] came, woke up everyone and, with guns at the ready, told them to pack. Ond of the soldiers encouraged to take as much as possible. Her father was guarded separately. Danuta's grandmother Maria was also deported accompanying her family of her own free will as she could return to Lviv.

Like many other Polish families, Grandmother Maria, parents Janina and Stanisław, Danuta and sister Basia, her senior by two and a half years, were taken with the first transport. They were put on a train made up of cattle wagons. The wagon had a hole in the floor, which everyone used for a toilet.

The train travelled slowly, taking a good dozen days, while making frequent stops. When the train stopped, local people appeared and offered food in exchange for items worth trading.

Although only four years old, Danuta remembers many dreadful images. Since early childhood and for long years thereafter, she feared the loss of her mother. At least twice, it seemed to Danuta her mother would be lost. She remembers crying, "Mama, Mama . . . " while her mother and many others rushed out of the train during the stops to seek water and food. Once she didn't return in time, and the train departed without her. Fortunately she caught up with the transport by taking the next train.

Danuta also remembers her great despair later in the Ural . . . when the Russians took her mother to a labor camp . . . She ran after her crying "Mama, Mama", a pillow in her hands and cried. The fear of loss of her mother stayed with Danuta for the rest of her life. Today, she considers that to be with her mother in United States is not only good fortune but a blessing.

Mother and daughter invited me to their home. There, they showed me a document of singular content. To quote:

"1939-1942. Saved from extermination in the years of severe need, captivity and exile by the grace of Providence and efforts of the Government of the Republic of Poland. Given asylum in the hospitable land of far Iran, on the Eve of Christmas Day, for the remembrance of that salvation, in this document we bear witness to the great, heartfelt bond of our feelings and we are reminded of our undying obligation towards our Motherland—to pay the debt of life by working with dedication and integrity for its greatness and good, to always share fraternal love with our fellow countrymen, to faithfully preserve friendship with the nations with which we have been brought together by fate, war and common misery, to show gratefulness to God not in prayer alone, but also in virtue.

Tehran, during the office tenure of President Władysław Raczkiewicz and the Government of General Władysław Sikorski, 24th December 1942. Delegate of M.P.i O.S. [Ministry of Labour and Social Welfare of the Polish Government in London]—Member of the [Polish] Parliament"

I asked questions and listened with great attention to Janina's answers, to very painful and difficult stories. Janina was recalling:

"With freezing temperatures minus 40 degrees, they brought us to a village called Kizel, in the Urals. We were assigned one room in a cottage. Danusia fell ill with pneumonia and without any spirits, we tried to apply cups of kerosene.[4]

The kerosene caught on fire that we managed to extinguish. Somehow, she came through. They separated my husband from us, who had to work in the forest, and we only saw him on Sundays. Later, he was imprisoned because he spoke in German and was believed to be a German spy. Each week, I brought him clean clothes and took his soiled laundry."

In June 1941, when Hitler attacked Soviet Union, even worse times came upon Poles in all the deportation locations. Defeats in the front forced the Soviet authorities to seek a coalition with the Allied forces. The most important result of the Soviet treatment of Polish deportees was the Sikorski-Majski agreement. On 30th July 1941, General Władysław Sikorski, the Prime Minister of the Polish Government in London, concluded an agreement with the Soviet government in Moscow, under which everyone was granted "amnesty". The deportees received *udostoverenie*, i.e. identity cards showing they were free to move across the country. Most of the deportees began to leave their locations in search of the newly forming Polish Army.

For a ration of potatoes, a local farmer took Janina, her daughters and their grandmother to a station in Kizel. From there, they went to Kazakhstan by train with a large group of Poles.

Stanisław Batorski remained in prison, and the family does not know what happened to him. For a long time, they cherished the hope that perhaps someone might someday tell them what happened to him . . . but no one ever had any news of him. [5]

In June 2016, thanks to the help of Dr. Andrzej Boboli form IPN, Warsaw, Danuta learned the date of her father death: May 16, 1942. She wrote me, "Finally I know when he died, most likely from disease and starvation, but the pain of knowing that I could not bury him, is overwhelming."

Both recounts and documents reveal that the migrations of Poles from the far ends of Soviet Union took weeks, sometimes months. Poles were seen at every railway station from which trains moved south and were the main source of information about their fellow countrymen and about the forming Polish army. General Anders[6], who was well aware of the situation, transferred the military recruitment points from central Russia to Uzbekistan. He believed that the only way at least a portion of the Poles could be rescued, was by evacuating them to the Middle East.

I asked Janina how she remembered that time.

"On leaving our deportation places, we were all left to our own devices. You could get some help if you had valuable things to exchange–valuable in the Russian reality: clothing, jewellery. These items could be exchanged for food. But after two years in Soviet Union, no one had anything left to exchange. Disease and hunger decimated people. Exhaustion killed them during that "migration period" across the vast expanses of Russia. Poles who managed to reach military facilities were utterly exhausted, often mortally ill.

"In Kazakhstan, we lived in a mud hut. The hut was limited to one entrance, and it had no windows. We slept on some straw spread on the dirt floor, and water often managed to enter our hut. We soon joined the group of the forming Polish Army. Our daily food source was minimal consisting of a piece of bread and a piece of sausage. I never touched that bread myself, but I gave it to my daughters. I never even mentioned this sacrifice to my mother, because that would make her worry about me . . . To survive, we searched for roots in the field . . . "

The influx of civilians coincided with the inflow of volunteers for the army. Polish soldiers shared their already meagre rations to support the incoming masses. The number of children from the army volunteer families was immense, and everyone joined in caring for them. The soldiers went from *kolkhoz* to *kolkhoz*[7] searching for Polish orphans and take them put of Soviet Union.

Thanks to the initiative of the Polish Embassy in Kuybyshev and General Anders, a kind of kindergarten/orphanage was created at each military center.

Children were accommodated wherever there was space, in Uzbek huts, in tents, and in sheds. Rough living conditions, lack of water, primitive sanitary facilities, and freezing weather caused an outbreak of typhus and dysentery, and many children died.

Under the threat of a growing German offensive and against the difficulties with procuring food, the USSR government agreed to evacuate the Polish army and civilians to Persia. General Anders issued the order to take each and every child, even if they had to be carried. Transports were to go from Krasnovodsk (current Türkmenbaşy, Turkmenistan) to the Persian port of Bandar-e Anzali on Caspian Sea.

The Poles were evacuated to Persia in two groups, in April and August 1942. The total number of evacuees was 116,131, including about twenty thousand children and young people. These deportees accounted for about a tenth of the people arrested and deported from Poland.

The Poles were brought from Bandar-e Anzali to Tehran by British GPT companies. The convoys also supplied the food needed during the transport of the refugees to Tehran.

I asked Danuta what she remembered from the evacuation.

"We were put on a ship and went with the army to Tehran in Persia. While there, my sister Basia and I were frequently ill, suffering with anaemia and whooping cough. I also had mumps abd double pneumonia.

"In Bandar-e Anzali, to seek food, Grandmother Maria exchanged gold for some bread. In Tehran, she came down with typhus and pneumonia, and soon died. She was buried in a mass grave at the Polish cemetery in Teheran.

"Poor Mama lost her mother, and her husband was interred in Russia. All she had left were the two of us—two little daughters. We were always sick with something, and she worried constantly.

"We were transferred to Isfahan. Basia and I were placed in an orphanage. The institution was run by the Daughters of Charity nuns along with their other institutions in Persia. Pope Pius XII provided funds for our institution to Daughters of Charity and the Lazarian Fathers. Mama worked in the orphanage to be closer to us. I loved to run in the garden, but I also remember my stay in Isfahan in the Armenian hospital with double pneumonia. There were not antibiotics applied, and finally my health improved. Later I was hospitalized with jaundice. My sister and I, it seems, spent almost all of our childhood in hospitals."

The children were taken from Isfahan to various places: Canada, the United States, Australia, New Zealand, Africa, and also to European countries, mainly Great Britain. Together with her daughters, Janina Batorska went to Mexico. Danuta recalls:

"First we went in buses to Mumbai and Karachi, then with an American military ship, we sailed across the Pacific to Mexico. I have pleasant crossing. I could not eat, and a young American sailor sat with me for hours until I finished my meal. Another sailor always played with the children. The ship was also used to transport Chiang-Kai-shek's soldiers. As a memento, one of the Chinese officers gave me a medallion inscribed in Chinese text, and also a booklet."

In the latter he wrote: "Na pamiątkę Małej i Miłej Dzidzia w drodze do Meksyku ofiarowuje 1943 (As a memento to Little and Nice Dzidzia on the way to Mexico—1943).

I asked Danuta why the Chinese officer wrote the inscription in Polish. Danuta replied that the Chinese officer specifically asked for the correct Polish words.

During 1943-1947, the three Batorskas lived in Santa Rosa, a colony of Polish refugees, in the central area of Mexico (near Leon). Danuta and Barbara went to school there and received their first Holy Communion and later were confirmed.

They showed me a bulletin from their archives: „Polak w Meksyku. Czasopismo dla osiedla i o osiedlu Santa Rosa. El Polaco en Mexico" (A Pole in Mexico. Periodical for and about Santa Rosa), issued on the occasion of a visit of the Mexican president, General Manuel Avila Camacho, to the colony of Polish refugees in Santa Rosa.

In Santa Rosa, the figure of a poet, Fr. Józef Jarzębowski MIC was very evident. I asked about him, and Danuta said:

"Fr. Józef Jarzębowski[8] made a great impression on me. His work and dedication to the Polish cause impressed me in particular. Before the war, he worked as an educator in the dormitory of the Gymnasium of the Marian Fathers in Warsaw. During the war, he escaped the Germans reaching Vilnius (where he met the Blessed Michał Sopoćko, confessor of St. Faustyna Kowalska). Then, after various turns of fate, including travel through Siberia and Japan, he came to the Marian Fathers in Massachusetts, United States in 1941. Learning of the colony of Polish children and of the Polish refugees in Santa Rosa, Fr. Jarzębowski came to us to Mexico. He worked in Santa Rosa as a teacher for seven years, and in his later life continued to enjoy interesting activities—he went to Britain, and became friends with Stanisław Radziwiłł[9]. He died in Switzerland in 1964.

"While in Santa Rosa, I read a book about Maria Skłodowska-Curie[10]. I was very impressed by the famous Polish scholar, and I remember deciding to do something meaningful, something creative in my life."

I asked about the Batorska's later life, after the period of Santa Rosa. Danuta said:

"In 1947, Santa Rosa was dissolved, and we had to manage on our own. We moved to Mexico City, where we stayed for three years. Fr. Jarzębowski organized a dormitory, and Mom worked there. I graduated from a Mexican school, completing an accounting course.

"Basia, my older sister, married and stayed in Mexico. She still lives there and is a successful painter. In 1976, Basia had an exhibition of her works in Warsaw. Her second husband, Gabriel Zaid, is a famous Mexican poet, who collaborated with Octavio Paz. I left Mexico for the United States in January 1950. My aunt, Jadwiga Watt, nee Batorska, sponsored my entry into the States. Her husband, David Andrew Watt Jr, a West Point graduate, reached the rank of colonel in the U. S. Army. I first joined them in Forth Worth, Texas, and a year later moved to Los Angeles to join Mama in 1951. I graduated from high school in Los Angeles and started my studies at the University of California, in Los Angeles (UCLA) where I studied Fine Arts. After earning my Master's degree in Fine Arts, I later was awarded my doctoral degree in Italian Baroque Art History. I consider the period of my studies in Los Angeles one of the happiest times in my life, comparable to my early childhood spent in the Białowieża Forest.

In 1970, Danuta Batorska became a professor of the University of Houston in the Department of Art, where for the next thirty years she lectured on the history of art. Professor Batorska writes articles on Polish art for many art journals in the States, in Italy and in Poland. Many of her academic essays concern Italian Baroque art. She is a recognized expert in the work of the Italian painter and architect Giovanni Francesco Grimaldi (1605/6-1680), and authored a monograph and cataloque raisonee on him.

After the death of her mother (Janina Batorska died in Houston in 1994), and on her retirement six years later, Danuta Batorska moved to Palm Desert in southern California.

I asked Danuta Batorska how she viewed her life, what does she thinks of America—the country where she finally settled down. She responded saying:

"God and faith helped me and my mother to survive, to leave the inhuman land . . .

"I try to help my students; I see that as a kind of mission. People with a past as traumatic as mine are lonely in America, as they are on their own. In the States, doctors are not familiar with such cases, or people with similar experiences. Only the Holocaust received public attention and serious study.

"What do I think of this country? The USA is a country that offers the greatest possibilities to a person who wasn't born here. Europe doesn't give such chances to immigrants, only America does, not Mexico, not any other country . . ."

NOTES

1. Białowieża Forest is one of the last and largest remaining parts of the immense primeval forest that once stretched across the European Plain. The forest has been designated a UNESCO World Heritage Site. It is home to 800 European bison.

2. Uhlans—Polish and Lithuanian light cavalry armed with lances, sabres and pistols. Uhlans typically wore a double-breasted jacket with a coloured panel at the front, a coloured

sash, and a square-topped Polish lancer cap, derived from a traditional design of Polish cap, formalized and stylized for military use.

3. NKWD—People's Commissariat for Internal Affairs was a law enforcement agency of the Soviet Union that directly executed the will of the All Union Communist Party. It was closely associated with the Soviet secret police, which at times was part of the agency, and is known for its political repression during the era of Joseph Stalin. The NKVD is best known for the activities of the Gulag and the Main Directorate for State Security (GUGB), the predecessor of the KGB. The NKVD conducted mass extrajudicial executions, ran the Gulag system of forced labor camps and suppressed underground resistance, and was responsible for mass deportations of entire nationalities and Kulaks to unpopulated regions of the country. It was also tasked with protection of Soviet borders and espionage (which included political assassinations abroad), influencing foreign governments and enforcing Stalinist policy within communist movements in other countries.(see: Wikipedia). In colloquial use, the name NKVD became a synonym for any and all crimes committed by the Soviets.

4. Cupping therapy is an ancient form of alternative medicine in which a local suction is created on the skin; practitioners believe this mobilizes blood flow in order to promote healing. Suction is created using heat (fire) or mechanical device (see: Wikipedia).

5. In June 2016, thanks to the help of Dr. Andrzej Boboli form IPN, Warsaw, Danuta learned the date of her father death: May 16, 1942. She wrote me, "Finally I know when he died, most likely from disease and starvation, but the pain of knowing that I could not bury him, is overwhelming."

6. Władysław Anders (1892-1970)—a general in the Polish Army, commanding officer of the Polish Army in the Middle East and Italy during WWII. Campaigning against both Germany and the Soviet Union at the outbreak of World War II (September 1939), he was captured by the Soviets and imprisoned until the Polish-Soviet agreement of August 1941. Allowed to form a Polish fighting force on Soviet soil from former prisoners of war and deportees, Anders soon had 80,000 men, but he realized that he had no chance of liberating Poland from the East with an army under Soviet control. As a result of both Polish and British pressure, Joseph Stalin allowed Anders to march into Iran and Iraq (1942). The Poles subsequently distinguished themselves in the Italian campaign, capturing Monte Cassino. A staunch anticommunist, Anders remained in Great Britain after World War II; the communist Polish government deprived him of his citizenship in 1946. Thereafter he became a prominent leader of Polish exiles in the West. (see: Encyclopedia Britannica).

7. Kolkhoz—a collective-owned farm, created by combining small individual farms together in a cooperative structure.

8. Fr. Józef Jarzębowski MIC (1897-1964)—member of the order of Marians of the Immaculate Conception, and a poet. For seven years, he worked in Mexico with Polish orphans in Santa Rosa and Tlalpan.

9. Prince Stanisław Albrecht Radziwiłł (1914-1976)—diplomat, chargé d'affaires of the Polish Government in Exile, delegate of the Polish Red Cross, director of Olympic Airways. One of the organizers of the Sikorski Historical Institute in London and founder of St. Anne's Church at Fawley Court.

10. Maria Skłodowska-Curie (1867-1934) - born in Warsaw was a Polish and naturalized-French physicist and chemist. She was famous for her work on radioactivity and twice a winner of the Nobel Prize (first woman to win a Nobel Prize).

Chapter Seven

Captive of the Theatre

Marion Andre[1]

In the program notes for Robert Shaw's play "The Man in the Glass Booth," there is a statement by the director Marion Andre. The simple, beautiful text seems to sum up his life's credo:

> "I AM"
> I am holder of words,
> They are dredged out from the river bed of my past, and like hard pebbles, rattle in my head.
> I am carrier of sounds. They are coiled in the long rod of total recall, and like baying hounds, take away my rest.
> I am catcher of smells. Once known to me, they are seeping through the pores of air, and like bitter acids, moisten my eyes.
> I am porter of stones. Spattered with blood, they are buried in the tunnels of my mind, and like heavy boulders, weigh me down to my knees.
> I am watcher of smoke. It is billowing from tall chimneys and like a black shroud covers my face, my hands and my life.

Born far away, son of Jewish people who are dead, survivor of the Holocaust, I am adrift on the volcanic sea of my memories, enclosed in the echo chamber of my pain.

What kind of man is the author of these words?

Marion's parents came from Poland's eastern region. His grandfather, a wealthy and respected man, was the only Jewish landowner in the district of Podole. His thousand-acre estate, not too far from the city of Tarnopol, was called "Nowosiolka Skalacka."

Marion's father, Emil Tenenbaum, was a medical student in Vienna, when he met his future wife Roza, a pharmacy student at the same university. In love, and wanting to get married quickly, Emil shifted from medicine to pharmacy, because the program was substantially shorter. Soon after their graduation, Emil and Roza married. After living abroad for a short while, the young couple returned to Poland, settling first in Skarlat, later in Lwów. Emil Tenenbaum acquired a pharmacy from Dr. Poratynski and he and Roza began their professional life together. A linguist, who was also well-steeped in ancient culture, Emil used to speak Latin with Dr. Poratynski's son, a pastime they both thoroughly enjoyed.

Emil, a great lover of literature, was an author himself. He wrote a few novels, among them The Backgrounds, which was published in Lwów, as well as a play "It Started with a Lie." Both works were well received by "Wiadomości Literackie" (Literary News), the leading literary magazine of its day. The year was 1931.

Marion was born in Le Havre, France, where his parents lived for a while. Back in Poland, his sister, Hanusia, was born when he was four years old.

Marion was taught languages from a very early age. His English teacher was a graduate of Cambridge. Marion fondly recalls the figure of his professor who was so enamored of Polish and English literature. When the Germans entered Lwów in 1941, Marion's teacher was walking down the street, a volume of Shakespeare in his hand. He was killed by a bullet from a German rifle.

A few months later, the entire Tenenbaum family found itself enclosed in the Lwów ghetto. Marion and his sister worked outside the barbed wire walls, collecting scrap metal used for a German company. Their parents had arranged the jobs for large sums of money—so the children could wear "WIRTSCHAFT WICHTIG" badges (Needed for the Economy). These badges were to protect them from round-ups. They did not, unfortunately, save Marion's sister. One evening when they were returning home to Korzenna Street within the ghetto, a military police vehicle pulled up beside them and tore the sixteen-year-old girl from her brother's arms. She made it as far as the concentration camp in Belzec.

A friend of the family's, a Major Resz, helped Marion obtain false documents. Marion changed his surname from Tenenbaum to Czerniecki. (He had the change legalized after the war.) With the help of Maria B., whose name will appear later in this tale, Marion managed to escape from the ghetto. His mother was rescued some time later. When they tried to reach Marion's father, it was already too late: the ghetto had been destroyed, the in-habitants killed or "transferred" to concentration camps.

Marion made his way to Warsaw. He had the address of two sisters in the Żoliborz district whose husbands—Polish officers—were prisoners of war. The women were harboring and assisting Jews. Marion stayed with them for two months. Then he found a place of his own. He does not have Semitic features, so he was able to move freely about the city.

He had many friends in Warsaw. He soon joined the underground, becoming a member of the Polish Socialist Party branch of the Home Army. He used the pseudonym: "Emil." When the Warsaw uprising broke out, he fought in the Old City. As Warsaw burned, he made his way through the sewer system back to Żoliborz. From there, after the defeat of the uprising, he was detained with others at the camp at Alten Grabow, in Germany.

Because of his knowledge of German, he was delegated to sort documents. Whenever he found a document giving someone's full name, he would hide it to prevent it from being deciphered, then pass it on to a higher underground official. The camp was filled with his comrades from the uprising; the Home Army organization continued its underground activities. One day Marion was summoned by his friends. They seemed preoccupied and upset. They began asking him questions:

"Where did you learn German? You're a Jew!"

"Yes" he answered calmly.

"Why didn't you tell anyone?"

"No one asked me."

They did not question him further. He was shattered by their changed attitude—their distance—to him. It was totally unexpected. After all, they had all been members of the underground; so much held them together. Despairing and in shock, he walked aimlessly, unaware that he was heading straight for the barbed wire fence. He simply saw nothing before him.

"Don't be an idiot!" he heard a voice say.

A friend, Zbigniew Korytowski, with whom he had fought in the Old City and Żoliborz, grabbed Marion's shoulder and pushed him away from the fence. "Don't be an idiot!" he repeated.

Marion remembered the time they had both fought in Warsaw. He remembered the sound of the shots, and how the defenders huddled behind sandbags, unable to stand it any longer, wanting desperately to flee. Then Korytowski had stood up and shouted: "Don't be afraid! Don't be afraid!" He had managed to restrain them all, to calm their fears with his words and his attitude.

After the war Marion travelled to Paris. Through the Red Cross he learned that his mother had survived the war, and that she was in Warsaw. He boarded a train and returned to Poland. There he learned the circumstances of his father's death. His grandfather had been shot in front of the orphanage he'd built for the children at Skalat. Of all Marion's close relatives, only his mother and his father's one sister had survived.

Long after the war, in Marion's new country, Canada, he would write of war and survival. These themes are the substance of his short stories, among them: "The Gates", "The Leave-taking", "The Saviour", and "Maria B."; and his plays "The Sand", and "The Aching Heart of Samuel Kleinerman". The latter is very reminiscent of the Polish play, "The Germans" by Leon Krucz-kowski. It deals with those moments when decisions which profoundly influence one's life must be made.

In the short story "Maria B.", Marion Andre piles image upon image, scene upon scene. The artist is quite evident here, as is the man of theatre who can illuminate certain events to make them stand out vividly.

The scenes and dialogues are fluidly eloquent. The story is extremely moving. It tells of a young man who escapes from the ghetto and makes his way to an address where he is to receive help. The woman who is to help him is called Maria. She is an extraordinary character: fascinating, full of life, happiness, shrewdness and cunning. At the same time she is noble and, in a simple, beautiful way, totally natural. Maria shares her flat with an old woman who is told that the young man is Maria's distant cousin.

The old woman does not believe this; she suspects the young man is a Jew. She badgers him, interrogates him, makes him swear by the cross that he is a Christian. Maria remains level-headed, playing the role of the joking, happy cousin, making light of the woman's suspicions, all the while knowing very well that she could report them to the Gestapo any minute. The woman is a threat. Maria keeps giving her vodka, knowing her weakness, till finally the old woman falls asleep. Maria and the young man still have a few hours before they are to begin a journey to another town. They have the following disturbing, memorable conversation:

I said: "Maria."

"Yes?"

"Maria, I think I won't go with you. I'll stay here till tomorrow morning and I'll go back. I'll need an armband. Perhaps you could help me make one. I'll get through somehow, I am going back."

Her voice came as if from a great distance. "Back? Back where?"

"To the ghetto."

"Don't be a bloody, cowardly, self-pitying fool!"

Maria shot back through the darkness. She leapt off the bed. I saw her walk across the room, to the door, an angry abusive shadow.

"She is an alcoholic! A sick woman! An ass! A bloody, vicious, sick ass! Are you going to commit suicide because of an ass?! There are many people like her."

"Maria," I said quietly. How am I going to avoid them all? You saw it for yourself. It's on my face who I am. I can't turn to Christ each time someone stares at me. I can't keep swearing to a lie. I can't! I can't!"

Maria yelled back. "You'll swear on the wounds of Christ every time it's needed! Only saints don't abuse His name. And I doubt that too! It's commanded: 'Don't kill.' And Love Thy neighbor.' Once broken, everything goes. I figure that the sin of false testimony, if you believe in sin, burdens the one who makes you commit it, not the one who commits it!"

"I once wrote:
The only stable element in our lives is the past.
The present is too blinding and chaotic.
The future's too fear ridden and dark.
"I know it sounds paradoxical; nonetheless I think it's true.

"You know, experience is supposed to enrich man, but my experiences have been so terrifying. So many years have passed since the war, yet they torment me still. I often think of my father. I can see his face. The pain is overwhelming.

"I realize I'm much of a loner, despite my friends, the people around me, and the work I love. Perhaps my war experiences have given me this sense of solitude. I once staged Bertolt Brecht's 'Man's Man' in Montreal. The play shows to what extent a person can change under pressure from those around him who push him in a particular direction. I'm aware that a so-called good man, under different conditions, can become a monster . . . I've lived through more than others have, I've seen more, I'm different. I've seen more because I've witnessed the debasement of man by other man.

"So much is said about Polish anti-Semitism, particularly on this continent. Undoubtedly there have been many instances of such a "creed," and many glaring examples of anti-Jewish activities: but these things are almost universal. Nevertheless, and this needs to be said over and over again, many, many Poles offered their help. My mother and I survived the war thanks only to the Poles. Both of us were hidden by Polish families. The children in the home where my mother hid used to call her 'auntie,' and they showered her with affection. We always recalled the figure of Maria B. with great emotion.

"It always bothers me when such a one-sided view of Polish people is suggested. I lived in a large city. Perhaps the situation presented itself differently in smaller towns where life was more difficult. I know that anti-Semitism existed in Poland, it would be foolish to deny it, but to speak of it as a part of the Polish "national character" is wrong! One should reject such wholesale condemnations. It is this type of sweeping generalization that is a curse of our times. As far as I'm concerned, I was shown a lot of goodness by Poles, those who hid me, and those who helped me.

People I stayed with often warned me, not directly but in a roundabout way, not to venture outside for evil things were happening in town. One thing I do know—man's ignominy has nothing whatever to do with his heritage. Baseness is an individual trait, not a national one!

"I remember once I was riding a streetcar. There were Germans on board as well. They were looking at me. I decided to get off. I was sitting next to a nun. Suddenly she took me by the arm and whispered: 'May God bless you, my son.' Her eyes were so full of sympathy and comfort. I remember them to this very day."

When the war ended, Marion returned to Poland and found employment with the Ministry of External Affairs. For a time the authorities sought out educated people, especially those with a knowledge of languages. For almost four years Marion was Second Secretary at the Polish embassy in The Hague. He married a Dutch woman, and they had a son, Tom. In 1949 Marion returned to Poland. Great changes were taking place then, changes for the worse, the country was turning toward Stalinism. Marion lost his job with the Ministry.

He began to write and soon found work with the "Kleks" Children's Theatre. He also wrote for cabarets, and published a play, "The Theory of Loyalty," which won an award in 1953. He translated Erskine Caldwell for the "Czytelnik" publishing house, as well as Caldwell's "Tobacco Road," which was staged by a Wroclaw theatre. Marion's own stories appeared in Przekrój and the literary monthly, "Tworczosc". Gustaw Holoubek's theatre in Katowice commissioned a translation of Eugene O'Neill's "The Hairy Ape" from him. At this time Andre was also in contact with Krystyna Skuszanka, the theatre director.

The times were difficult, and the terror of Stalinism loomed larger. Marion's marriage faltered. He divorced his wife, who returned to Holland and remarried soon after. Their son remained in Poland with Marion. In 1955 Tom went to visit his mother in Holland and did not return.

***

Roza Tenenbaum's brother, Marion's uncle, had survived the occupation of Warsaw. In 1945 he had made his way to Italy, and a year later to Canada. In 1956 he sponsored his sister, Roza, Marion's mother. One year later Marion himself came to Canada, arriving in Montreal and then asking for permission to stay. Soon after, his first wife and her husband immigrated to Canada. Tom, Marion's son, was re-united with his father. A few years later Marion remarried and had a second son, Krystian. The family settled in Montreal.

After his arrival in Canada, Marion worked for several months as a lamp salesman. Later he got a job as a proofreader with an English publication geared to the Jewish community. This occupation forced him to perfect his already admirable knowledge of English. Every day he taught himself new phrases, particularly American slang, repeating each phrase aloud. He applied for and received a job as a stage manager in a local theatre. The producer, sensing Marion's knowledge of theatre from his astute observations, said to him one day: "Maybe you'd like to try your hand at producing?" The play was Tennessee Williams' "Summer and Smoke." Marion took the stage name Marion Andre, from his two first names, Marian Andrzej. Soon he was offered a second directorial assignment. The year was 1958. The productions were well received by both critics and audiences. At the same time Marion wrote his first North American play, "The Scorn of Fate," based partly on a story by Jean Paul Sartre. He wrote it in English, and sent it to the French language section of the CBC in Montreal. Within three months the play had been translated into

French and was broadcast. The English version was aired only four years later.

In Canada, it was extremely difficult to make a living at such endeavors, particularly at that time. Marion remembers renting an apartment, and being asked by the landlady:

"What do you do for a living?"

"I'm a theatre director and I write."

"Yes, but what do you do for a living?"

In 1964, Marion established a theatre troupe called Freelancers, which was one of the first English-speaking professional theatre groups in Montreal. They appeared at the Theatre Club, a 250-seat house with two resident troupes, performing alternately in English and French. Many of the actors had other employment as well, but were pleased to have the opportunity to appear on stage. Around this time Marion met Charles Rittenhouse, the head of the English department of the Protestant School Board in Montreal, who offered him a position as Drama Specialist in the local secondary school system. The job was important also because it brought in a steady income. Marion also worked with a group of McGill University students, staging several plays, among them Jean Giraudoux's "Tiger at the Gates" and Max Frisch's "The Firebugs." The Freelancers put on "Antigone", "The Lark" by Jean Anouilh, and Shaw's "Mrs. Warren's Profession."

The then YM/YWHA hired Marion to conduct theatre classes and direct plays. His production of the Goodrich/Hackett dramatization of "The Diary of Anne Frank" was particularly successful.

Marion wrote steadily through this period, producing among others works "The Fate of a Poet," which was based on documentary evidence from the trial of Soviet writer and dissident Josef Brodsky. The play was taped by CBC radio and became the first broadcast of its type in Canada.

In 1967, when the Saidye Bronfman Centre was established in Montreal, Marion became its first theatre director, later taking over the direction of the entire centre. He stayed at this position for six years, until 1972.

The Holocaust was the central theme for the 1971/72 theatre season. One of the plays to be produced was Robert Shaw's "The Man in the Glass Booth," a work already staged in London, New York and Tel Aviv.

The play, a dramatization of the Shaw novel of the same title, is a fictional account of the celebrated Eichmann trial in Israel. The play's central figure is a German Jew named Goldman, whose wife and three children perished during the Holocaust. After the war Goldman becomes a New York millionaire. On the surface, he is a hard, ruthless man, but he is also a man obsessed with memories, and a feeling of guilt for having survived the concentration camps. The play opens with Goldman returning home, carrying a newspaper with the headline: "Pope Forgives the Jews." Goldman, incensed by the story, "transforms" himself into the Dorff (Eichmann) figure for an as yet undisclosed need of his own. Israeli agents, suspecting Goldman is in fact Dorff, whom they are seeking, kidnap him and place him on public trial in Jerusalem. During the trial, Goldman obsessively plays the role of which he is suspected. His aim is to secure a forum that he may display the conditions which form the basis for fascism. During his trial speech, he says of Nazism as a supposedly purely German phenomenon, "People of Israel, if he (Hitler) had chosen you, you also would have followed where he led."

This is the central moment of the play, the realization that Hitler could have been born anywhere, that a madman capable of influencing vast numbers of people can be found anywhere.

The representatives of the "Survivors of the Holocaust" association, who were to sponsor the production, demanded to see the script. Shortly thereafter they announced that the play was offensive; it smacked of anti-Semitism and they would not allow it to be staged. Despite a lengthy public debate over the play and the insistence of a number of persons that such a demand would constitute censorship, the association's decision to ban the play was upheld. So as not to cause a conflict in the Jewish community.

Marion Andre expressed his opinion on this issue in the "Montreal Star":

Shaw's central message is that people must continually be on guard against their own weaknesses which make them follow where tyrants want to go. This warning has been deliberately travestied to make it sound insulting and anti-Semitic.

He went on to call the play's cancellation . . . an outrage . . . an act of coercion . . . the curtailment of freedom . . . One cannot block it at home and demand that it be restored elsewhere.

Marion eventually left Montreal, accepting a teaching post in the Drama Department of York University in Toronto, where he and his graduating students staged Jean Paul Sartre's "The Trojan Women."

When Andre realized that "nothing happened" during the summer months at the St. Lawrence Centre in Toronto, he decided to establish his own theatre. Such were the origins of "Theatre Plus." Marion has said:

"I saw this building (the St. Lawrence Centre) standing empty and silent and my need to continue working in the professional environment took over. I was warned by many people that such an ambitious theatre program during the summer would not succeed in Toronto, but I couldn't believe that people's intelligence exists only in winter and dies out in summer."

"Theatre Plus" was established at the St. Lawrence Centre in 1972. Its raison d'être is indeed ambitious.

"To produce plays from the national and international repertoire which reflect and illuminate political, social and moral problems of our times."

Three years later, a critic for the "Globe and Mail" would write: When Marion Andre came from Montreal three years ago, he was determined to establish himself as a theatrical contributor of note in Toronto. The Polish-born director was smart enough to recognize that the city's theatrical barricades were unguarded only in summer, for Torontonians still believed that everyone went 'to the lake' in warm weather. (September 11, 1975)

At first three plays were produced each year, then four, and now five plays. Marion always tries to include one Canadian work in the season's repertoire. Though the initial years were "heart and back breaking" says Marion, the results are quite spectacular; it now seems difficult to imagine cultural life in Toronto without "Theatre Plus." The works staged always deal with some aspect of the problems of contemporary society. Productions that provoked a strong response from both audience and critics alike were. Tennessee Williams' "The Glass Menagerie", starring American actress Carol Teitel, and "A Streetcar Named Desire"; John Guare's "The House of Blue Leaves", a tragicomedy on the con-temporary American psyche; Christopher Hampton's "The Philanthropist"; David Rube's "Streamers", a bitter account of the Vietnam war; Pam Gems' "Dusa, Fish, Stas and Vi", the story of four woman in conflict with a man's world; Clifford Odets' "Awake and Sing", Preston Jones' biting satire on the Ku Klux Klan; "The Last Meeting of the Knights of the White Magnolia"; Ernest Thompson's "On Golden Pond"; Jean Anouilh's "The Lark"; Henrik Ibsen's "A Doll's House"; George Jonas' "Pushkin"; Michel Tremblay's "Forever Yours Mary Lou"; and Friedrich Durrenmatt's "The Physicists."

All the plays presented by "Theatre Plus" focus either directly or indirectly on the concerns and problems of contemporary society. Here's a sample of critical opinion of "Theatre Plus" offerings.

The presentation of "The Lark" is superb . . . Andre is the man who brings to Toronto plays that make the brain work, the heart throb and sometimes the belly quake with laughter. (McKenzie Porter, "The Toronto Sun")

Nothing is forced or false. Andre's touch (in "The Philanthropist") is light but firm throughout. The result is stunning. (Myron Galloway, "The Montreal Star")

. . . the interplay between the play's racking hilarity and its deep sadness, between its flourish and its dying moan, is what makes ("The House of Blue Leaves") so exhilarating. Marion Andre manages the play's trickiness most adroitly. (Urjo Kareda, "The Toronto Star")

. . . taut, provoking . . . a stunning production (of "The Physicists") under Andre's meticulous direction which balances the humor and the drama on a fine fulcrum of irony. (Myron Galloway, "The Montreal Star")

That is both the strength and the weakness of Theatre Plus that it is inextri-
cable from its founder and artistic director Marion Andre. That makes it provocative, brave (what other theatre proclaims a mandate to do plays of "political, social
and moral importance"?), intelligent, peppery, touchy, defensive, irritating, and
rarely offering anything that doesn't provoke an argument—of one kind or another. More than most theatre people, Marion Andre is passionate, an evangelist
for his kind of theatre. (Gina Mallett, "The Toronto Star", May 1, 1982)

Marion Andre is the dynamic artistic director of Theatre Plus, Toronto's
summer stage. He is something of a maverick, with several first Canadian
productions to his credit and a driving belief that what's happening on the
stage should be a simultaneous reflection of what's going on outside the theatre. (Linda Kelley)

Andre has said of his role as artistic director:
"I tap society's unconscious—that's the role of an artistic director."
And one critic has added:
"Andre has some decidedly unpopular opinions. He believes, for example,
that the plays most worth producing are those which stand for something."
Marion Andre often speaks out on the role and character of the theatre, in
particular, the specific nature of cultural and theatrical life in Canada. In the
Winter 1979 issue of Canadian Theatre Review, there is an interesting conversation between Andre and Pierre Caron de Beaumarchais on contemporary theatre,
particularly the theatre in Canada, entitled "Dialogue Fantastico:"
MA: " . . . Gestures, modulation of speech, these are all a part of Theatre . . . But this is not dramatic action. As I said before, people go to the
theatre to look at themselves. To recognize themselves in action. And therefore, a director has to bring that forth. Make people who sit comfortable in
their chairs . . . "
CdeB: "In other words you are advocating an 'engaged' theatre. 'Theatre
engage,' as your modern compatriots call it—am I right?" I ventured carefully.
MA: "Yes, yes, yes. Theatre which is devoted to Life. Theatre which does
not shrink away from interpreting social, moral, even political problems of
the times. Theatre which has the courage to shout to people—'See, this is
wrong and this "wrong" is of your own making. It is in your power to change
it!' Yes, Theatre, which is as merciless in the evaluation of Life as a flood-
light directed at an object standing in darkness, every detail beautiful or ugly
is under scrutiny. Theatre of purpose!"
CdeB: "Why not stick to the beautiful only?" I said. "My God, there's
enough ugliness in the world as it is. Why look at it on Stage?"
MA: "To sharpen your awareness of it. To pinpoint the responsibility, I
repeat, beautiful and ugly. They are of equal importance, as 'without one you
cannot recognize the other.' Yes, theatre of great issues, but not this bag of

pseudo-amusing imbecility, this heap of 'merde,' which most of your writers and producers . . . "

Marion Andre holds a unique position in Canadian theatrical life. He attained this position on his own, through his talent and efforts.

He lives in a lovely home. His study is filled with books, cacti and rocks. He considers rocks nature's finest sculptures. Rocks and cacti can survive the worst, most adverse conditions. In the centre of the room there is a large clay bowl filled with water. The rocks in this bowl will never lose their color. The room also contains theatrical memorabilia and papers. A photo of his parents stands on Marion's desk.

His face is fascinating; intense, ascetic, with delicate features and expressive eyes. A face one never forgets. The face of a still young man.

He is friendly, sincere, yet all the time maintaining a certain distance. The time he spends with others is indeed a gift to them. He is a fantastic conversationalist and listener. He has survived much, yet there are no traces of cynicism or bitterness in his character. He is an artist, an aesthete. His stories are artistically presented images. They exude certain mysticism. One thinks of him as a man full of love and at the same time despair.

His third wife, Ina, is a woman of remarkable beauty. She is a dancer and teaches movement at Ryerson Theatre School. Together they have raised Marion's two sons, and Ina's children, Jennifer and John. Marion says Ina is a unique human being, a woman of intuition and understanding; he says he owes her very much. Their union is a very happy one for both of them.

One of his sons, Tom, lives in Quebec City. He is a photographer and sculptor. The other, Krystian, winner of the Governor General's Gold Medal for English, is on scholarship in West Germany studying comparative literature.

He deserves to be proud of his life and satisfied with himself, for he has accomplished so much, despite having seen and survived so many horrors. He is still full of ambitious ideas and the energy and need to create.

He has lived in his new country—Canada—for almost thirty years.

I have strong ties with Canada. When someone asks me if I feel Canadian, I reply firmly: 'Yes!'

"I remember getting off the plane in Montreal, and seeing my mother and uncle there to greet me. We drove home in the car. It was seven o'clock in the morning, and neon signs were still flashing brightly. I had this inexplicable sense of safety, freedom. Those blinking lights gave me courage, and a feeling of elation.

"Many people here don't appreciate the value of this great chunk of land: one can say what one wants and, given talent and persistence, one is sure to get ahead. This is still a land of great opportunities.

"America—the States are powerful, filled with opportunities, intoxicating . . . and yet . . . Canada seems to have a better balance. To my mind, greed is the worst trait a man can have. It will make him stop at nothing.

Sometimes it seems that greed is worshipped in the U. S. to excess; it's like a motor, an energy which relentlessly—and blindly—drives a person.

"Only in Canada can a party like the NDP thrive. There is a continual search here, an attempt to balance all the country's problems—industrial and social. This is seen in the conscious effort to create multiculturalism and bilingualism. Such an approach is most valuable and rather rare in other countries. It creates conditions which make me feel a part of the whole, and, as a result, con-tent. I had an offer from New York—I knew there were great possibilities there—yet I turned it down, realizing, of course, that if one makes it there, you're at the top.

But that's not my attitude to life. I need to create with a broader purpose in mind . . . I need to share . . . You could say that this sounds like a Christian attitude. I have a statue of the crucified Christ, which I brought back from Mexico. People ask me what I keep it for. I don't know . . . it has great significance for me; it expresses man's suffering born of his own need. And it's artistically beautiful.

"I think of Poland in specific images, which appear to me suddenly: Jastarnia, I'm sitting on some stone steps; it's evening; and the Baltic is rolling gently. I used to spend hours staring at the water. Another image is Zakopane; skis, my dog; a German shepherd: I would be skiing downhill, he would come bounding down after me . . . And the people - only their faces. I react very emotionally to all this, to all the memories. My son once asked me if I would go back to Poland. No. I'm afraid of the emotional shock . . . Nonetheless I often have these flashes of events I experienced or seen.

"I wrote a poem, 'I Thought of You,' about something that happened to me one rainy Warsaw day. It's a kind of lyrical memory. The ending goes:
How could I forget it?
Even though it happened a million years ago, on the street of a city where you remained and I have left a city that gave me the first taste of love, a city that lives inside me, yet the one
I will never see again, the incident with you how could I forget it?

" . . . Now, at the moment, I'm very active in Canadian life. I have a strong urge to speak out, and I do. My one great satisfaction is that I'm able to work in the theatre, and to write . . . What do I lack? . . . Perhaps my mother's love. She passed away in 1963.

" . . . This country is very young. Cultural needs are a very low priority. First there is the need for bread. When I came here twenty-seven years ago, things were very different from the way they are now. There was one theatre in Toronto, now there are twenty-five. After New York and London, Toronto is the largest theatre centre in the English-speaking world.

"What is theatre for me? I've been associated with it for a long time. The first play I ever saw was 'Shouting China' at the Grand Theatre in Lwów. I remem-ber the great Polish actor, Stefan Jaracz, a friend of my parents'. I remember a scene from my youth that took place during the war: one day there was a round-up on a Lwów street. I was taken too, to Janowska Street, to the transit camp. I was there for one night, and all of the next day, then I was released. I don't know why, perhaps because of the 'WIRT- SCHAFT WICHTING' badge. I have one particular memory of that time: people huddled together; barbed wire all around; puddles after the rain. It was evening. A few hundred people, among them a rabbi, deep in prayer. From across the field came the whisper of a doctor offering the prisoners poison: 'I've got cyanide.' He was suggesting suicide. Then suddenly I heard a clear voice above all the others, it was an old Jewish actor reciting part of King Lear . . . Religion, human weakness, theatre—those are the three alternatives: seeking and understanding God, accepting suffering, escaping from it or extricating the meaning of pain, in order to give it significance. The scene shook me. That allegorical, almost biblical scene probably formed a great part of my education.

"What is theatre for me? The study of the human soul.

Or, to quote Arthur Miller, "The stage is the place for ideas, for philosophies, for the most intense discussion of man's fate." In short, theatre is the examiner of public and private mores, an instrument of self-awareness, an instrument of social concern, an instrument of social change.

In Canada such a concept, though gaining in the last twenty years, still lacks sufficient strength to move theatre from the periphery to the centre of social and cultural life.

Marion Andre wrote in the June, 1983 Canadian Forum:

We are still in the fold of the early North American tradition that pegs theatre chiefly as a medium of entertainment. It falls into the category of non-essential concerns—is even seen as a luxury. Such an activity stripped of its intrinsic spiritual value, guided solely by the laws of supply and demand in the marketplace, becomes first and foremost a "commercial commodity."

When theatre is placed in that category it necessarily lowers its artistic sights, delivering goods that are digestible and easily marketable, carefully avoiding subjects that probe deeply, smack of controversy or carry a message of a disturbing nature.

This tendency, to a degree reduced during the period of explosive growth in the fifties and sixties—and coincidental^ during the time of Canada's solid economic expansion—is back in fashion again, induced, no doubt, by the present inflationary woes and economic uncertainties.

"Commercialize or perish" is the battle cry of a number of theatre critics and entrepreneurial gurus; "play the wares of low-brow entertainment and higher aspirations be damned!"

It is sufficient to scan the repertoires of the major companies from across the land. They are crammed with frolic froth, dotted with a most narrow range of classics, and sweet-sprinkled with an occasional Canadian work—

conspicuously free of any purposeful, valuable examination of the contemporary condition at home and abroad.

Naturally, one should not assume that all theatres in Canada follow such a route. There are some that manifest their understanding of theatre's role by consistently and steadfastly producing works of social, moral or political coloration. But, for the most part, the accusation stands. Our "key regional theatres" seem to lack the will and conviction to enter boldly into the twentieth century. They quite zealously and, I suspect, deliberately, shy away from the challenge of reflecting the ills, the problems and the prospects of our day.

For me, social justice is the foundation upon which society builds its future.

If this consideration is not entrenched in political thinking—I believe that sooner or later rebellion against unjust conditions occurs and society gets torn asunder.

Yes, social justice is the most crucial ingredient of our lives—or rather, it ought to be if we want to "live happily," in fact, if we want to survive.

Not agreed which, in the final analysis, is the motive to expand one's material wealth, not the quest for power which most often is the propellant in political life—but the desire to do away with hunger in the world, with oppression (be it of the left or the right variety), with social injustice . . .

Yes, this is the credo by which I live. I once wrote a poem and I cannot shake off the images contained therein; maybe because of that—in whatever small way I can effect a change—I try to do so, in my private life, and naturally in whatever I can through theatre.

"When I turned fifty, I wrote the following poem:

"1921 — 1971"
I am fifty years old. Half a century presses hard within my ribs,
half a century like a cause-way connecting two shores; one already distant and
hazy, the other invisible, yet approaching.
Half a century of twisted roads, littered with incidents and events, all of consequence at the time, now faded
or indistinguishable, except for a few
that like cliffs against the empty sky
or gallows on a silent square remain sharply etched, irreducible.
Half a century
of loose fragments; toxic childhood, pre-shortened youth, maturity nurtured on
masquerading and running.
Half a century of losses (mostly), ruined homes, shattered hopes,
and wakeful nights only rarely lighted by the fireflies of happiness.
Half a century
that future historians would call "stupendous"
because some men set camp on the Moon,
but for me, and others like me
the half century of shame,

because of
camps
barbed wire
famine
mass flights
the unending
scream
of the tortured the deafening silence
of the executed."

In September 1989 Marion Andre sent me[2] his letter published in "Globe and Mail" (Toronto, September 25, 1989.

LIFE SAVED BY POLES

I am a Jew and survivor of the Holocaust, I am compelled to contradict Israeli Prime Minister Yitzhak Shamir, who. As you reported on September 9, apparently stated in an interview that Poles are anti-Semitic from birth, that "they suck it with their mother's milk". This is something that is deeply imbued in their tradition, their mentality" (*Poles Born Anti-Semitic, Shamir Says*). I need to say with passion that I am alive today because of the help of several Polish Christians.

During the German occupation of Poland, I escaped from the ghetto in the city of Lvov. I was assisted by a Polish Christian man who supplied me with forged documents and a Polish Christian woman who helped me reach Warsaw by accompanying me on the train. I lived in Warsaw with three Polish Christian families who were aware of my origin and were proud to have me in their homes in spite of the fact that a verdict of death might be their fate, because such was the Nazi policy for those who concealed Jews.

The woman who helped me become a "free" man also saved my mother. She helped her cross the barbered wire fence border of the Lvov ghetto and brought her by train to Warsaw, where she arranged for her to stay in the home of a Polish Christian family. My mother was treated with loving care by those people of low income, and lived there in hiding until the collapse of the Warsaw uprising in 1944. Then she and the family were moved by the Germans to a small town where she survived the war and came to live in Canada.

Was there anti-Semitism in Poland? Yes. Many Poles despised the Jews. I witnesses and suffered occasionally from their prejudice as a teenager. I am certain such people still exist there as they exist in other countries. But to say that the whole Polish nation was/ is like that is false.

Not all Poles were/are Jews haters. Therefore I rebel against such a preposterous generality as the one expressed by Mr. Shamir. That is the reason for this letter. To fulfill my need to speak in defence of the Polish Christians who risked their lives to save Jews.

What I have said should not be interpreted as a concession of those who believe the Carmelite convent should remain on the site of Auschwitz concentration camp (the Vatican said is should be moved). That place should be left intact as a memorial to Jewish martyrdom. And as a gruesome reminder to what level human cruelty can soar where the counterforce – the sense of brotherhood, love and justice – stays silent.

Marion Andre
Founding Artistic Director
Of "Theatre Plus"
Toronto

***

In writing he was always using the Holocaust, the central experience of his life, as the main theme. He published novels: "Maria B." (Mosaic Press, 1990) and "The Battered Man" (Mosaic Press, 1996).

Marion Andre passed away in Toronto on May 9, 2006.

NOTES

1. The part of this chapter appeared in 1984 in my book titled "Dreams and Reality. The Polish Canadians Identities" sponsored by the Ontario Ministry of Citizenship and Culture and the Adam Mickiewicz Foundation of Toronto. In Polish the book appeared under the title "Kanada, Kanada…", in Warsaw, 1986.

2. Marion Andre wrote me the letter: Sept. 27, 89. He used form" Oleńka" - my Polish nick name for Aleksandra.

Dear Oleńka,

I think you'll be pleased to read my letter to the Editor (enclosed). I thought of you writing it! How are you, and your son? I haven't heard from you for such a long time! Are you busy? Happy? And do you plan to visit my continent at some point of time?

It would be interest you to know that "Maria B," will be published, after all! By the end of this year I will have the book in my hand, and a copy will fly to you as soon as possible. And another interesting thing – a few days ago an unexpected visitor knocked at my door. He and I met during the Warsaw Uprising (we were fighting in the same unit), he read about me in your book, came to visit his son who lives in Winnipeg, and his nephew who lives nearby Toronto- and he came to say "hallo" to me! We had a lovely time talking to each other. I was trying to reconnect with those "old days", but I couldn't equal true precision of his recollections, his memory was working so much better than mine. And another troubling point – he spoke to me in Polish and I had such a difficultly to respond fluently! So many words got lost in my mind! So many phrases were unclear, convoluted! Any way…

Please drop ma a line, will you?

With everlasting affection,

Marion

Ina sends her love.

Chapter Eight

Angola-Born, Brazil-Based Poet, Artist

Tomasz Lychowski

I met Tomasz Łychowski in Warsaw in 2010 at the presentation of the book *Moja droga na księżyc* ("My Way to the Moon"). A tall, handsome gentleman with a gift of listening to his interlocutor. Later I would discover the same sensitivity in his poems. He told me, "There is a saying in English, *Let bygones be bygones.* I prefer to look back through the haze of time. It makes the past look more romantic. Less hurtful".

He was born in 1934 in Portuguese Angola in Africa, in the town of Nova Lisboa. His Polish father, Tadeusz Łychowski, an agronomist, was born in Kiev. His mother, Gertruda Seefeld, was German. She was born in a little village Chorinchen near Berlin, in a peasant family. What brought them to Angola is hard to say, perhaps, in Tomasz's words, "circuitous paths of heart".

Tomasz remembers the natural beauty of Angola, his fondness for its inhabitants and for *pirão* (a local corn specialty), but also the nasty symptoms of malaria and the bitter taste of quinine. He also has memories of the journey to the port city of Lobito and of the ship Niassa, which in 1938 brought him and his parents to Europe. A year later, the war broke out and his parents joined the underground resistance. His father was a member of the *Stragan* (The Stall) group,[1] to which Ludwik Kalkstein also belonged, and Tomasz remembers that Kalkstein came to his parents' apartment for clandestine meetings. In August 1942, upon the betrayal of Kalkstein who turned out to be a double agent, the Gestapo jailed in the Prison nearly 200 members of Armia Krajowa (Home Army), among them Tadeusz and Gertruda together with their 8-year-old Tomasz.

Today, Tomasz Łychowski has already celebrated his 80th birthday, he is most likely the youngest surviving prisoner of the Pawiak prison. [2]

He remembers that every morning at six there was a roll call. Female prisoners, lined in double rank, reported in German. Tomasz recalls that after a certain time this duty fell on him; he reported, *"Fünfundzwanzig Frauen und ein Kind (Twenty five women and one child")*. To that, the Commandant retorted, *"Fünfundzwanzig Frauen und ein Man (Twenty five women and one man"*, and, pleased with his own joke, burst out laughing.

After the roll call, they were given "breakfast" (he describes it as "some kind of slop and a tiny bread crust"). For "lunch", they got a little bit of watery rutabaga soup. When hunger pangs made him cry, his mother shared her portion with him. Until they were transferred to a "laundry cell", Gertrude and Tomasz slept on the floor, half-leaning against the wall, because in a cell which held twenty five women and one child, there was hardly any room to lie down even for a handful of people. As bad as the lack of space was, the fear of air raids was even greater. Guards had safe places to hide, but the prisoners were locked in their cells where they shook in terror every time they heard the unmistakable whoosh of falling bombs. Oftentimes they fell quite close by.

Gertruda who was fluent in German wrote petitions to the prison commandant on behalf of the inmates. Once she submitted a petition to let Tomasz visit his father at Christmas time (Tadeusz was kept in a solitary cell which meant he was considered a "high value" prisoner.) That Christmas visit to his father in a Pawiak solitary cell, however brief, was an intense experience for the child. The underground continued to be active even in prison. The women of the Pawiak were able to conceal a note with important information in a loaf of bread. Tomasz remembers how he trembled during the inspection: he was searched, but no one thought to cut through the bread. During the visit, his father showed him a glass shard which fell into his cell during one of the air raids. Possession of any sharp object was strictly forbidden in the prison: it could have been used as a weapon against guards or else to commit suicide. From the distance of time, Tomasz sees the profound symbolism. Why did his father show him that glass sliver? Perhaps he wanted to assure his son that even in prison he still had a measure of control over the situation. The same with a letter to Gertruda and Tomasz from Auschwitz in which he wrote that the Łychowski family motto was, "Be gentle with the weak and tough on the strong". "Being tough on the strong" made it possible for him to survive Auschwitz and Buchenwald.

On April 23, 1943, after nine months of investigative detention, the Gestapo let Gertruda and her son go free. Five days later, Tadeusz Łychowski was sent to Auschwitz. Next time Tomasz saw his father was in 1946 in Antwerp; by then he was 12. For him, both parents were heroes. "My brave mama, says Tomasz, "it must have been hard to be German in Poland during the occupation; she was often viewed with suspicion or even overt hostility. She did not attempt to leave for Germany and wait until the war ended. She stood by her Polish husband and joined the resistance. After the war she received a commemorative medal of the Armia Krajowa."

In 1995 Tomasz visited Warsaw and donated to the Pawiak Prison Museum the Christmas card which cellmates of the cell #25 gave him for the holidays. He remembers, "That Christmas was happy times in the Pawiak. Our cellmates managed to make my day even more special in an extraordinary way. Along with the holiday card, I received a toy bunny made from a piece of fabric. I have it to this day. Through our Ukrainian guards, Wanda Samardak smuggled a pair of boots. When we were arrested in August, I was dressed in short pants and sandals. This was clearly woefully insufficient. Wanda Samardak was a saint incarnate. Her serene presence was enough sometimes to ease up the tense atmosphere in the cell. She was taken to a camp and perished there. I often think about them all and I thank the Lord that they were a part of my life."

He emphasized the role faith played in his life, "I still can hear the plea from a woman during an airstrike in besieged Warsaw. We were hiding in a cellar, bombs were falling all over the place. I was 5, and I was scared. Suddenly, a woman, an utter stranger, cried out at me, "Pray!" She must have thought that the prayer of an innocent child might save us all."

After the war, in 1949, Tadeusz and Gertruda, together with 14-year-old Tomasz, left for Brazil. UNRRA[3] made it relatively easy to emigrate from the war ravaged Europe to South America. Brazil seemed a good choice, since they already knew Portuguese. Tadeusz, an agronomy engineer by education, planned to work in tropical agriculture.

On board of an old English vessel *Charlton Sovereign* they set off from Bremen to Brazil. The journey lasted almost a month, instead of scheduled ten days: in the middle of the journey the ship started filling up with water and eventually careened to one side. To balance it out, the captain gave an order for everyone to shift to the other side of the vessel . . . The ship carried nearly 800 emigrants, including young children. Food was becoming scarce, and the risk of sinking was ever growing. Eventually, they made it, but barely, to Vitória, in the state of Espírito Santo, where the ship underwent some repairs. Local journalists showed up, and Tadeusz gave them an interview. The effect was immediate: kind-hearted Brazilians started bringing them food, and for several days the sad saga of the passengers was all the Vitória citizens cared about.

When the ship was patched up, they continued their journey to Rio de Janeiro. Guanabara Bay left them speechless, as did the magical cityscape of Rio de Janeiro. He recalls, "Upon disembarkation, the local official asked every male passenger, "*Fala português*? Do you speak Portuguese?" "*Sim,* Yes", only my father was able to respond. And because of this, he was promptly . . . arrested. It turned out that the captain sent a cable to Rio that among his passengers there was a dangerous communist agitator who spoke good Portuguese. Evidently, Tadeusz's interview in Vitória did not sit well with the captain. After several days spent apart, everything was straightened out, and Tadeusz Łychowski, who survived the Pawiak, Auschwitz and Buchenwald, was free once again. This time in Brazil."

After only one year in Brazil, Tadeusz Łychowski passed away. He was 52 year old, and, according to Tomasz, "What he went through in German camps shortened his life dramatically. Grief-stricken, mother and I lived for some time very modestly in provincial Brazil".

Tomasz went to school for the first time when he was 15; he entered the grade school as a home-schooled student, while they still lived in a small provincial town Vassouras, in the vicinity of Fazenda Secretário. In 1952, he and his mother moved to Rio de Janeiro where he enrolled in high school evening classes. He finally finished his studies, after many fits and starts, when he was already in his thirties, with a degree in English from a Cambridge Examination Centre (CPE and DES) in Rio de Janeiro, and subsequently, also in Rio, from the Pontifical Catholic University. He mastered three languages: Polish, English and Portuguese. He worked in education, including higher education, developed teaching methodology, and lectured. He also contributed to *Aproximacões,* a magazine published in Brazil by Professor Henryk Siewierski. He made an emphatic note that Henryk Siewierski represented "the brightest example of vivid Polish presence in the cultural life of Brazil." Siewierski is a Literature Professor in *Universidade de Brasília,* the founder of the Norwid Department in the same university, poet, writer, and translator.

The *Aproximações (Convergence)* magazine was published for several years by Henryk Siewierski and successfully served as a bridge between Polish and Brazilian cultures. Tomasz also translated and wrote for other Polish publication, such as *"Lud" ("People")* in Curitiba, Brazil, "*Głos Polski" ("Voice of Poland")* in Buenos Aires, Argentina. When asked to compare the Polish Diaspora then and now, he responded that "unfortunately, the Polish Diaspora is gradually crumbling. The peak years were during and immediately after the war when large political emigration that counted perhaps several thousand people landed in Brazil, Argentina and other South American countries. During the war years, the *crème de la crème* of Polish poetry gathered in Rio de Janeiro (Tuwim, Lechoń, Wierzyński); sculptor August Zamoyski also belonged to the same circle, as did actor and director Zbigniew Ziembiński, other writers and intellectuals and even the composer of "Red Poppies on Monte Cassino" Alfred Schütz. A sizeable group of Polish aristocracy arrived to Brazil on a ship named . . . *Angola.* Later, Brazil closed the doors on the wartime immigration, and a number of war and postwar immigrants relocated to different countries. With time, those who remained started, as they say in Portuguese, "passing over to the better world". *Partir desta para a melhor.* He muses that *"Lud"* in Curitiba closed, the readership of *Głos Polski* in Argentina is declining, and "Sunday services in our little Polish Catholic Church in Rio attract just a handful of worshipers. It is the only time a week we have a chance to converse in Polish. Father Zdzisław Malczewski, Rector of Polish Catholic Mission in Brazil, publishes *Echo Polonii Brazylijskiej ("The Echo of Polish Diaspora in Brazil")* in Polish and *Polonicus* in Portuguese. He is fighting a valiant fight trying to bring Brazilian affairs and Polish culture closer together."

A quote from his book was used for this exhibit, *Malarstwo to wielka radość, à la mozartiana, gdy wulkaniczne otchłanie poezji stają się trudne do pokonania... (Painting is the greatest joy, like Mozart's music, when volcanic abysses of poetry are hard to overcome . . .)* He published several books of poetry in Portuguese, English, and Polish: *Glimpses/Vislumbres* (1996), *Voices/Vozes* (1998), *Brisas/Powiewy* (2000), *Graniczne progi/Limiaresde fronteira/Thresholds* (2004), *Encontros/Spotkania* (2006), *Skrzydła/Asas* (2008) and, most recently, *Recome ç o* (2014).

Tomasz Łychowski's great passion is poetry and art. He participated in individual and international shows. In Poland, he showed several dozens of his paintings at the exhibit in the Staszic Palace in Warsaw. The show was titled "Polish Traces in Brazil: the Art of Tomasz Łychowski". A quote from his book was used for this exhibit, *Malarstwo to wielka radość, à la mozartiana, gdy wulkaniczne otchłanie poezji stają się trudne do pokonania... (Painting is the greatest joy, like Mozart's music, when volcanic abysses of poetry are hard to overcome . . .).* He published several books of poetry in Portuguese, English, and Polish: *Glimpses/Vislumbres* (1996), *Voices/Vozes* (1998), *Brisas/Powiewy* (2000), *Graniczne progi/Limiaresde fronteira/Thresholds* (2004), *Encontros/Spotkania* (2006), *Skrzydła/Asas* (2008) and, most recently, *Recome ç o* (2014).

He remembers that he printed his first book of poetry "My Parnassus" with his own hands on a mimeograph. He was happy that from those youthful poems which he wrote at the age of twenty, one was selected for a publication in the collection *Recomeço (Starting from the Square One")* which he published in 2014 in honor of his 80th birthday. First, he wrote in Polish. Later, English became his professional language. The volumes *Glimpses/ Vislumbres* and *Voices/Vozes* were written in English. Currently, he writes mostly in Portuguese. In a radio program with Maria Wieczorkiewicz for the Radio Polonia, he accepted her idea that what he writes is Polish, while what he paints is Brazilian. He says, "This proves once again that an immigrant possesses multiple identities". He also wrote the above mentioned book of memoirs, "My way to the moon". The Polish original and a Portuguese translation *Meu caminho para a lua* were published in 2010; an English version in 2012. In it, he intertwines the stories from his own life. When

asked, if this book of reminiscences talks about who he is, about his childhood in Angola, he responded, "My book reveals the core reason why I keep
wandering around the world. Uprootings. But everything, of course, had
begun in Angola. It is still alive in me."

ENOUGH !
(Tomasz Lychowski. Translation from Portuguese Graham Connell)
Am I to blame
- born in Angola -
for not being black?
Adopted by Brazil
for being a gringo?
Guilty?
For being the son of a German in Poland
of a Pole in Germany?
Enough of false guilts!
Won´t the true ones suffice?

                                              ***

This is what he says about his wife, "Krystyna was born in Rio de Janeiro
in 1941. Before the war her mother, Anna Schulz, was a rising start of the
Polish ballet; her father, Jan Schulz, served as an adviser at the Ministry of
Interior and was a prominent jurist. His father-in-law's last name was German, Schulz; his mother's maiden name was von Sendbusch. In 1939, Jan
Schulz was among those who organized the evacuation of the Polish government to Romania. In the turmoil of war, the young Schulz couple was separated, and only by miracle they reunited later in France. They arrived to Brazil
by the way of Portugal and suffered, like almost everyone else, the early
vagaries of immigrant life."

THE MORE
(Tomasz Lychowski. Translation from Portuguese Graham Connell)
The more I seek Brazil
the more I discover Poland
—and the other way round
The land and the spirit that dwells in her
speak out
Cherries and mangos
birch trees and guatambu
the blond child and my grandson
curumin
Truly
I feel a Pole
Brazilian

When man
shows his human face
when he crosses the threshold
of himself
when he stretches out his hand to me

***

I asked him what his ethnic identities - Angolan, Polish and German - are based upon. He responded, "Not ethnicity or nationality, but a meeting with a human being "who extends his hand to me (and I to him!). Not ethnic, but human affinity. Enough with "we and they". But deep inside, I am Polish. As Shakespeare put it, "in the end truth will out".

NOTES

1. Stragan—General code name "Stragan" or the "Stall". Polish intelligence organization of the Home Army operating in Poland, the Czech Republic, Austria and Germany.

2. Pawiak-prison. During the World War II German occupation of Poland, it became part of the German concentration-death camp apparatus in Warsaw.

3. United Nations Relief and Rehabilitation Administration (UNRRA) was an international relief agency, largely dominated by the United States but representing 44 nations.

Annex

Literary Journalism, Storytelling, or Literature of Fact [1]

Writing belongs to a world of magic; many of us would like to take up residence in it. Mere membership in this club is rich in experience—and teaches humility. Good writing is the marriage of elegant form and interesting content. When the telling of a story is as good as the story itself, it usually results in good literature.

Each one of my books is in own way different, as well as in its literary form. Each time I wrote as if I were reacting to a reality, people and events around me. Other people's stories about their lives always interested me. I always listen to them with interest and sometimes I even want to write about them. My own life provides me with enough emotions that often become my inspiration. I write about the good and the not so good and this is a form of therapy for me, when I share my thoughts and observations with others. I want to understand my life and the world around me. In writing I come close to and in some way I adopt new and unknown phenomena. I keep learning to live, like everyone else, stumbling not only once, not twice….

We write in order to present facts and share our insights, feelings, sentiments, and experience. The need to write may arise for many reasons; one hopes that, it springs from a need to share something we find important.

My thoughts on what I understand about writing are my own and need not be validated by the ideas of others. This is my own standpoint: I regard writing primarily almost as a mission, as a service to others, but also as a service to myself and to all things that I hold dear, that I admire, that fascinate me and that I simply love. Sometimes I say to myself, "I hope I live long enough to read calmly, listen, take notes, think and, finally, write it down".

… How do I choose my protagonists? How do I find subjects that interest me? My interlocutors seemingly appear of their own volition. I meet them in Warsaw, Gdansk, Krakow, Torun, Opoczno, in Canada, in the United States, and even in Argentina and Brazil. Usually I describe how we have met at the beginning of my stories.

When I took up a residence on this side of the ocean in 1990, I met, among other people, WWII-era immigrants. For many of them, settling in a foreign land presented a set of problems, painful acclimation and difficult adjustments to a new life. They dealt with it by throwing themselves with passion into local Polish affairs: they founded churches, organizations, charities, newspapers, books, and bookstores.

Often times, when I listened to their stories, I almost had to "bate my breath"; I do have a soft spot for stories that "melt my heart". And if a person who tells me a story does not nurse a painful memory, hold a grudge or feel sorry for himself, I tend to respond with greater warmth. I ask questions, and I listen. Afterwards, I suggest to them that I write about it—without ever knowing if it will turn out to be a short story, interview or a longer piece of prose. We would agree that they tell me everything, exactly like it was, and later I offer to have them vet the text. I would remove the fragments from the narratives that were intended for my ears only, and not for the whole wide world. This is their sacred right, and I have a duty to act ethically.

LITERATURE OF FACT—CREATIVE NON-FICTION

Right from the start, the 21st century has been, and by all accounts will be, the age of the literature of fact. Step into any Barnes and Noble store: the first things you see are monographs, biographies, autobiographies, criticism, memoirs, diaries, interviews, interpretations, and reports.

Contemporary readers expect a book to be well documented. They are greedy for facts and first-hand experiences. They struggle to comprehend the world which, through television and the Internet, intrudes into our lives and overwhelms us with its dilemmas, problems, catastrophes and penury. The world turned out to be a great unknown, and we strive for more knowledge and deeper understanding of our surroundings, or at the very least we want to understand them just a little better. Additionally, we Poles and our friends and kin, want to know more about affairs related to our history and our national heroes, but also about an average citizen with whom we tend to identify. We are seeking new insights into our history, even though we are aware that „history likes to repeat itself".

The term *creative non-fiction* (also known as *literary non-fiction),* may sound a little contradictory. The word „creative" points to the fact that an author employs methods and techniques usually reserved for fiction writing.

In other words, he or she practices the art of crafting a narrative with the tools and strategy of a storytelling.

Creative non-fiction is rooted in the 20th century, in the tradition of literary journalism; Ernest Hemingway, who sent dispatches from travels in Africa to such magazines as *Collier's Weekly* and *Scribner's Magazine,* practiced this particular brand of journalism. The Swahili word „safari" entered the English vocabulary through his reporting. Hemingway wrote his stories in the first person, from his own point of view.

It was a new approach to telling a story; previously, the dry and dispassionate „general journalism" was divorced from the personality of an author. It presented facts and named names, but did not attempt to acquaint the reader with an actual person or with his or her unique identity.

Eventually, many other styles of narration emerged. In the 1970s, so-called *literary journalism* reigned supreme: authors strove to present the point of view of an ordinary person. It became possible to write about monarchs and presidents in an entirely new way. One could read about their feelings, dreams, passions and misfortunes … as if it were a novel; yet it was essentially a work of realism, the people in these pieces were real characters with real names. Once this method was adopted beyond journalism, the label *literary journalism* was no longer accurate. At that point, the term *literary/ creative fiction* came into use.

Non-fiction authors have a special contract with readers: we do not make things up. Everything we write about is based on documents, facts, corroborated eyewitness accounts, and it is the author's responsibility to make sure that a reader understands it. I believe that, these basic ground rules notwithstanding, the field for creativity is vast.

Why do writers choose to write non-fiction instead of fiction, if there are so many strict conditions and inviolable boundaries?—Because a story based on real facts and events is full of energy and emotional charge. True stories teach us what it means to be righteous, brave, or scared. They introduce us to unusual characters, and since they were—or still are—genuine, and existed in real life, it makes them even more compelling. They win the readers' trust, and it is a writer's responsibility to keep this trust unbroken. It does not always happen the way it should.

In 2003, James Frey published a book *of creative non-fiction* "A Million Little Pieces". The book is a brutal collective portrait of drug addicts whom the author met in rehab clinics. In a nutshell, he shows a searing human drama full of unusual characters, conflicts and tensions.

Oprah Winfrey selected "A Million Little Pieces" for her "Book Club", the book became a bestseller and made the author rich. Many people found it inspirational.

But soon enough the truth emerged that the book was not based on true facts and true people.

The book was fundamentally a piece of fiction; Frey invented both events and people. Three years later, in 2006, journalists began exposing the lies, unraveling one claim after the other. In the end, it was clear: nothing described in the book had really happened. Oprah Winfrey and the public were indignant; the author faced legal charges.

James Frey later explained that he had tried to interest a publisher with his book, but the manuscript was rejected. After he presented it as a true story based on his life, the books was accepted for publication.

***

I call my non-fiction texts "stories", they have a loose structure, free-flowing narrative, and they can—but not always—be longer than a short story or shorter than a novel. There may be multiple angles to the story, and voice may be given to multiple opinions. The narrative in first person offers the story from the point of view of a protagonist and preserves his voice and his take on the events. The use of the third person allows a lot of additional information, including the historically accurate data derived from primary sources. I employ both techniques, though I prefer to make my heroes speak for themselves, using their own vocabulary and voice.

If writers choose the literature of fact as their craft and their genre, they realize soon enough (and with time, this realization only grows) the nature of the task at hand. First of all, writers must carefully observe that the basic facts of the story are accurate—the place and time of an event, as well as the cast of characters. The choices the protagonists make, their motivations, their lives, their luck, tragedies and pain, errors, disappointments, decline, but also joy and contentment—all must be credible. There are many different ways to show your protagonist, his destiny and his milieu. The challenge is how to tell the truth, be it "my truth" or that of the other person.

Is there one truth?... This is a complicated question. Every person has his or her own truth. Melchior Wańkowicz wrote in his last book that if you go around the table and ask everybody who drinks wine from the same crystal decanter, each person will see the reflected light differently: pink, green, gold, blue. "La Fontaine's Decanter" shows it from the point of view of each character. In what colors you see the reality often depends on "where you are sitting"... Does it mean that there is really no absolute truth, and how does the idea of respect for another opinion, for example, come into play?

The creative approach of a writer is reflected in a choice of a perspective which, like a camera lens, allows one to linger and to zoom onto a certain detail, to train the focus in such a way that will attract a reader's attention. It is these details that pull readers into a story, and set the gears of their imagination in motion. Silence also plays an important role in a narrative. It creates drama and tension. Saying "too much" breaks the tension; verbosity ruins the text. The writer must write in a way that is close to him or her. Generally speaking, as in any other literary genre, it is paramount that the writer is able to engage readers, to pull them into the flow of the story.

There are many things about which I do not know much; the same goes for a reader. As a rule, if in the process of writing authors discover that they do not have enough information about the place and period of the described events, it is their responsibility to make sure that the reader understands that.

A narrator writes in the first person, but also intertwines into a story excerpts from other people's testimonies, lends voice to concrete persons, shows their standpoints, reaches for their memories, recollections. The author also seeks to use documents, published memoirs, historical records, photographs or drawings.

I draw from various sources, and I later show various characters in a book. I used drawing in "Kaya, the Hero of the 1944 Warsaw Rising"[2]. I consult historical records, but I also seek advice and recommendations from others. I appreciate if a bibliography contains references to unpublished materials and archival collections.

My heroes let me use photographs from their private collections. Quite often, these images are a true photographic record of the era (such as the images of the Warsaw Uprising from the collection of Wiesław Chrzanowski), sometimes they are downright unique (eg. Jan Bułhak provided the photographs of his famous grandfather, Bohdan Bułhak). These images offer a wonderful local and period backdrop for the described events.

I make good use of archival materials. Some Polish archives, e.g. Central Army Archives (Centralne Archiwum Wojskowe -CAW) in Warsaw, several times sent materials directly to my home address. I was able to access the IPN (Institute of National Remembrance) collections on my visits to Warsaw. I have had very good experience with the American archives. *National Archives Collection College Park* in Maryland granted me free use of their images, among them portraits of Native American cryptographers, for my book "Open Wounds: a Native American Heritage". They not only gave me permission to use them in the book, but also mailed me high quality copies.

The Polish and American archival institutions allowed me to use materials from their collections free of charge; the Swedes and Brits acted differently. When I was working on a short text about my husband's cousin, Ingrid Bergman, I needed to check the dates of birth and death of numerous members of the extended Bergman family (I only had information on Ingrid's father, Justus, and Norman's grandmother, Blenda), I turned to the National Swedish Archive in Stockholm. They were ready to provide the necessary information, but charged significant fees for it. I was treated similarly at the British Imperial War Museum when I requested permission to publish two photographs of the planes piloted by Władysław Sikorski in my book "The Second Battle of Monte Cassino and Other Stories".

FINDING THE RIGHT TONE

When I write about a real person, I must present the information about the time and place of the events in such a way that will get my reader interested. One method is to "wrap it in mystery", to keep the reader in suspense; or else, one can "introduce unease", to appeal to poetic or philosophical sensitivities.

I call this process "a search for a tone", and I try to find the right one for every one of my stories. It may be a straight forward, linear narrative; it may resemble an old Polish *silva rerum,* a multigenerational chronicle, with its wide range of themes, change of atmosphere and poetics, with a complicated plot line, and the use of personal recollections. The style that one chooses can be compared to a garden—it can be manicured and ordered, or free-spirited and unrestrained.

A tone means finding the proper atmosphere, rhythm and language for each individual story. Certainly, I would want to write differently about Poles whose lives were forever altered by World War II, differently about Native Americans, entirely differently about my cat Suzy, or about my husband's cousin, the famous actress of "Casablanca" fame.

When "Ingrid Bergman and Her American Relatives" (2013) was published, Tomasz Wojtkowski, a singer and songwriter, wrote to me that the style of the book reminded him of a bossa nova. I liked this phrase, because from the very beginning I intended to maintain the warm, sincere and restrained tone for this family tale. I am attaching an excerpt from the letter, an unusual piece of literary criticism:

"After a quick preparation—I brewed myself a large mug of tea, emptied an ashtray of yesterday's cigarette butts, cleared the dirty clothes off the armchair and changed into comfortable, loose-fitting clothes—I delved again into the book about Ingrid Bergman.

For background music, I chose a bossa nova by Astrud Gilberto. I am not sure why and how I decided that this particular music style was the most appropriate, but it turned out I hit the mark. I always thought a bossa nova was a very peculiar type of song. It does not require a great voice. Its rhythm is very basic, and the performer almost deliberately subdues a melodic line. It is as if the songwriter went the extra length to avoid any musical excesses. But, in the end, they are all beautiful... In addition, the tradition of this understated singing makes the tune linger in the air like pipe smoke. Suspended in the air, it fills the entire space with its beauty and warmth. I am not talking about the warmth of a Brazilian beach (although this association is also valid, for obvious reasons), I am talking about this pleasant tingling in my chest linked to the feeling of relaxation and solace. These songs are about love, falling in and out of love, about dreams and journeys, about beautiful girls and their boyfriends. Exactly as in your book. When I read the book, I fell under the spell of this calm, warm, steady voice that told this family story. Like a talk with a friend at the kitchen table.

Yes, I selected exactly the right music for the reading.

"Ingrid Bergman in Private" is a book version of a bossa nova, and it does not matter that its main character comes from a cold country by the frigid sea; and that another character, auntie Blenda, with her high-neck buttoned-up dresses, wire-rimmed glasses, pressed lips, stern look and a Bible on her night table does not resemble at all that girl from Ipanema."

To continue with a musical metaphor: when I wrote about Roman Rodziewicz, a soldier serving under Hubal, I sometimes engaged, poetically speaking, "the whole orchestra": a tambourine, a flute, a violin. I wrote about Polish settlers in Manchuria, in the Eastern Borderlands, in the Auschwitz and Buchenwald concentration camps; and about the hard, difficult post-war years. I became a witness to an emotional meeting: Roman and his pre-war fiancée Halinka met for the first time many years after the war ended. They could not stop talking, trying to figure out how it happened that they had lost each other.

The narrators have an obligation to control their emotions and to present the events and their analysis in the most objective and temperate way. But sometimes, you like a character in a story "more … or less". It happened to me when I wrote about Ingrid Bergman. Well…must admit I was not a big fan of either of her Swedish husbands, but I had a soft spot for the Italian one, Roberto Rossellini. I consciously quoted from one of the books on Bergman. It was not my own sentence, but I attached it almost happily. I also quoted from a letter by Ingrid's aunt to Norman's father, on the same very subject. Blenda Bergman also had a strong opinion, which I was almost pleased to include.

RIGOR AND DISCIPLINE

What are the obstacles to writing? Dozens of daily distractions, people, "the entire world conspires against the writing". We are cognizant of how much has already been written, and how much is being written still, that at times it seems we are drowning in garrulousness… Yet, at the same time, it is a beautiful and noble thing when you can share something important with others.

Writing demands great dedication and discipline. Sometimes it happens—especially in a moment of crisis—that everything else except the writing, seems more important, more pressing. Perhaps it is often true. It is imperative then to be able to quiet that inner voice of distraction and interference, the voice which can become, quite simply, our enemy. This voice may pester us, it may ask "for whom—why—what for?", may tempt us with many interesting distractions. Laziness, too, urges us to watch yet another TV program –you may not even be all that much into it—or to surf the net, or to take a nap, or to talk on the phone, for the hundredth time about the same things.

Reading is a great ally of writing. I always remember what the philosophy professor Władysław Tatarkiewicz wrote in his "Notes to an autobiography": instead of hanging out with the same crowd and repeating the same words, it is better to sit down with a book.

When I write, I am usually alone—depending on where I am—with a sheet of paper, notebook and computer. Do I "see a reader before me" when I write? Yes and no. I concentrate, first and foremost, on being able to focus on, to bring closer or make clearer my chosen subject. In full honesty, I will get to know my reader a little later.

I do like meeting my readers after a book comes out. I appreciate these opportunities. A special contact with readers develops, they share their observations, they confront me with questions. Sometimes they really amaze me with their curiosity, with their desire to reach for something I could have missed or misrepresented. It is always a "good lesson" for me. I also value special friendships that sometimes develop between me and my readers.

Writers must be emotionally involved in the subject, but control their feelings. I like to say that emotions animate my writing, but I always put the text aside, let it "rest". After sometime, I go back to it and touch it up, refine it. I clean the text of emotionally charged fragments which tend to sound particularly abysmal with time. I like Hemingway's advice: "As a writer you should not judge. You should understand."

The more difficult the subject is, the more imperative it is to be economical with words, to be reserved, to avoid adjectives. The more important it is, the more understated the delivery should be. The reader must evoke an emotional response in the process of reading. The author should avoid offering ready interpretations. It is important to maintain rigor and discipline, particularly when one develops a difficult or delicate theme. The subject has to be presented in such way that a reader draws his own conclusions. That they hold their breath. The author must refrain from writing a ready commentary; it is reader's responsibility to be moved, to be surprised, to be puzzled, to use their head, to think… If it does not happen, it means I have failed.

Sometimes I write about the fates of families broken up by wars, or about individual dramas. An American publisher wrote to me that a reader identifies with these individual lives, they move him; and this response occurs because I do not insert my own commentary.

I remember the tragic flooding of New Orleans when around the clock TV channels showed nothing but horrifying images of the disaster: houses submerged under water, distressed people gathered up on roofs and waving their hands in hope of being rescued; a horse struggling with rising water. I remember a news anchor saying:

—On the left you can see a dog that is still alive and is desperately trying to remain afloat...

I wanted to tell him, "Don't say anything, I can see it, your words are superfluous..."

A STORY WITH A TWIST

I like it when something "unexpected" happens in a story, when I can spring a surprise on the reader. In "Kaia, Heroine of the 1944 Warsaw Rising" I recall the story when she and her friend managed to avoid death at the hands of Ukrainians only because of the help from a woman -a Ukrainian woman.

When I interviewed Zdzislaw Starostecki, I was surprised to learn that during one of the early battles at Monte Cassino, a German helped him tend to the wounded. I was happy to be able to quote this recollection:

"I saw on the ground two wounded field engineers. I dashed to them with the individual first-aid kit, but when I saw that one of them had a very serious abdominal wound, I felt despondent: with a handful of bandages I would not be able to help him. The wounded man was half-conscious. When I raised my head, I noticed that among the ragged rocks above us someone was waving the Red Cross banner. Next to it, I could see a German helmet. I waved my hand to him and invited him to come down and, before long, we ministered to the wounded side by side. The German had a fully appointed kit bag and was well familiar with first aid protocols... When we finished dressing the wounds, he snapped his bag shut and handed it to me without a word. Stunned by the gesture, I only was able to shout "Danke!" before he disappeared among the rocks. Without turning his head, he only raised his hand in acknowledgement. He was the first Wehrmacht soldier whom I met on a battlefield since the 1939 Battle of Kock. His humane gesture shook me profoundly".

Joanna Synowiec, a character in my story "A Better Day Has Not Come"[3], told me that in a Fergana camp in Uzbekistan, a Russian woman took a liking to her younger brother. Joanna said that the Russian could have simply taken Henryk from them. She also told me something that I value greatly, "But she was not a bad woman". I am enormously grateful to her for this phrase, because it added a new dimension to the text.

ETHICS AND SENSATIONALISM

When we write about real people, we enter into a special contract with ourselves—with our sense of justice, our code of ethics. I consider this point important.

Let's imagine that someone is writing about us—and writes things that are false or misinterpreted, a piece of gossip, or an untruthful and malicious assumption. No doubt, most of us would experience pain, shame, protest or anger.

Written documents can be quoted and referenced, but working with someone else's oral recollections is a separate and serious issue. It is paramount to be very careful when citing the words of our interlocutor who trusts us and to whom we owe a responsibility to not harm, blindside, use, or deceive. A writer must strive to behave ethically and must resist the temptation to sensationalize.

When I pose questions, I want to know more—ideally, "everything"; however, this does not mean that I will be able to use this "everything" later on. An interlocutor in good faith may say more, give more details, name more names, and tell more about his or her feelings—sometimes very intimate ones. There are encounters and moments when the interlocutor does not hide anything, does not censor his or her words, feelings, and memories, he or she shares them freely.

It does not mean that the writer will describe them all later, "for the benefit of the world". Our confidants deserve our respect, deference and tact toward their lives and privacy.

A trusting relationship with a writer is cultivated for years. Several years and several books later, the reader should be able to trust the writer. But the writer must be very careful and double check everything as much as possible. One should not trust one's memory, or the memories of interviewees.

Even authorized texts may contain excerpts which have escaped the attention of writers and their heroes. It is necessary to double-check everything whenever possible. It is really easy to fall into the trap of *mythomania*. Someone's version of events may seem to him or her true and trustworthy. But in reality, when people repeat the same story for years, they tend to embellish it, changes it here and there and ends up believing in the "gospel truth".

What are writers supposed to do when there is no way to verify information or there is a conflict in different accounts of the same event?—They have a responsibility to write about it, a reader has a right to know it.

The question of copyright is taken very seriously in the United States; I experienced this first-hand while working on my books. Every statement ascribed to a character in a book has to be validated by him or her; every lengthy quotation from a book has to be used with the permission of the author or from the publisher (if the author is no longer living). Of course, it is fine to use a brief quote, no more than several sentences; it is called "fair use". Still, my editor at the Purdue University Press told me of several pending court cases around the issues of fair use. Therefore, one must be very cautious.

I had an astonishing experience with my "cat" book "On the Road with Suzy: from Cat to Companion". It included email letters from my friend Ewa on the subject, among others, of a dying cat named Latik. Ewa had read the Polish version and had no objections. The American publisher requested a written statement from Ewa that she agreed to the publication of the letters.

—But there are no last names in the book,—I tried to reason,—there are only pets' names and first names of their owners.

—Doesn't matter. Please ask this particular Ewa, whose letters you use in the book, to send me a statement that she knows that these are her letters and that she knows that they are being quoted.

Ewa, a well-known scientist, author of several books and a professor of an elite American school, knew "what it was about", and without hesitations sent the statement of consent for publication.

WHAT ARE THE HONORS OF A WRITER?

I, for one, find letters from readers, meetings with them, and stories I hear from them all very moving. Also important are book reviews and literary awards. Someone told me once, "You can pray for reviews, but never ask for one". Every one of us, writers, awaits reviews, write-ups, and recognition. Every author is waiting for an analysis of his or her work and hopes for being noticed and acknowledged.

I remember well how much Melchior Wańkowicz cared about reviews, how laboriously he harvested every sentence and every citation. Even at 80, when he enjoyed a very well-established reputation—"of a national prophet", as he liked to quip—he was anxious about reviews. There were plenty of them. Nowadays, years later, all the voices from the archive of the author of "Herb at the Crater" ("Ziele na kraterze") shine anew and, tempered by time, they shine perhaps even brighter.

The above mentioned Wańkowicz had only one reward: that is, his readership. Other fellow-writers were very jealous of his popularity. Sometimes he would say—with bitterness, not with pride—that he never received a single award. He did not belong to any group, and was never singled out. He paid the price for his independence and for being "team of one", "his own man" I wrote at a greater length about it in my book about Wańkowicz.[4]

Here I just want to make one point: a literary award is a dream of any writing person... even if he wouldn't admit it... even to himself.

A book award is a recognition of the years of work, research and complete immersion in the subject; long years of solitude in front of a paper sheet (or, more likely now, in front of a computer monitor), long hours and days full of struggle with procrastination and nescience; years of pushing other things aside, meetings and often many pleasures, big and small.

To write means to dedicate hours to work which does not always reflect the enormity of our efforts and hopes, and quite often it brings us alienation, rancor and desolation. Writing means hours of loneliness that eventually stretch into years. Read writers' biographies, you can learn a lot from them.

We owe them so much. How many books helped us through the difficult times and heartache. The books that move us, dissolve us in tears or make us laugh remain with us forever.

When we encounter a meaningful book, we learn from it something new; it stretches our horizons, it changes our opinions and our mind, it broadens our viewpoint, it allows us to approach a subject from a different perspective, it raises our awareness, it elicits introspection, it brings hope.

A MESSAGE FROM ISAAC B. SINGER

When in 1985 I, as a Fulbright scholar, had a chance to talk to Isaac B. Singer in New York, he taught me a wonderful lesson on crafting a narrative, on "hooking" a reader. During our conversation, I asked him if there was anything he would like to say to young writers. Here is a fragment from the authorized text of Singer's answer:

". . . What is my message to men and women of letters?—That they meet three conditions.

"Firstly, have a story to tell. The present day literature is increasingly careless about that. It is important for the story to have a beginning, a development and an end. We do not need necessarily to adhere to Aristotle's recommendations, but it is, nevertheless, imperative for the writer to weave his story well. A consuming desire to get published makes writers forget their artistic mission of having to describe human experiences.

"Secondly, have a passion, a need to tell a particular story versus another one. I remember a time I had a good theme but no passion, so in the end I wrote nothing.

"Thirdly, it must be "my" story, a conviction that no one else is able to describe it so well. It is not easy to have such a conviction. It only comes to the greatest of writers. It is important to write about what one is familiar with, knows best; to have one's own story, one's own subject-matter.

"As for myself, for instance, what I know best are Jewish people, not those living in Sweden though, but those in Poland. We all have our limitations, our constraints. One should be able to realize that. I am not able to describe everything. It took me years to understand that. Initially, I wanted to imitate Knut Hamsun. I eventually learned that I was neither Tolstoi nor Hamsun, nor Gorki, that I must write about my milieu. This realization developed eventually into quite a private passion of mine."[5]

I quoted Singer's words in the beginning of the book "Kaia, Heroine of the 1944 Warsaw Rising". His list of three imperatives for writing is timeless.

NOTES

1. Published in: "The Polish Review", vol. 62, no. 3, 2017, pp. 79-90.

2. These drawings are made by a central character in my book, Cezaria Iljin-Szymańska: Dzungaria, 1920-1922; trip for honey to to an beekeeper in Zaysan; an NKVD hospital in the Ostashkov camp; and the NKVD Camp No. 41 in Ostashkov.)

3. Aleksandra Ziolkowska-Boehm, "The Polish Experience Through World War II: A Better Day Has Not Come" (Lanham MD: Lexington Books, 2013, ISBN 978-0-7391-7819-5, 2015), ISBN 978-1-4985-1083-7. Foreword: Neal Pease.

4. Aleksandra Ziolkowska-Boehm, "Melchior Wańkowicz Poland's Master of the Written Word" (Lanham MD: Lexington Books, 2013, ISBN 978-0-7391-7590-3). Foreword: Charles S. Kraszewski.

5. Aleksandra Ziółkowska-Boehm, „Korzenie są polskie", Warsaw 1992, ISBN 83-7066-406-7; The Roots Are Polish", Toronto 2004 ISBN 0-920517-05-6. Foreword: Major General Bruce J. Legge.

Index

Adamczyk, Wiesław, 85
Adamkiewicz, Jerzy, 8
Anders, Władysław, ix, xii, 96, 97, 100n6
Andre, Ina, 111, 116n2
Andre, Krystian, 111
Andre, Marion, Czerniecki, „Emil", viii, x,
    xiii, xv, 101, 102, 103, 104, 106, 107,
    108, 109, 110, 111, 113, 115, 116,
    116n2
Andre, Tom, 111
Anouilh, Jean, 107, 109
Attlee, Clement, xii
Avila Camacho, Manuel, 98

Babiński, Wacław, 8, 15
Bach, Johann Sebastian, 78
Bandera, Stepan, 91n2
Baptiste, Jean, St., 10
Barrette, Antonio, 16
Bartkiewicz, Adam, 54
Batorska, Danuta, Danusia, viii, ix, xiii,
    xiiin2, xv, 93, 94, 95, 96, 97, 98, 99,
    100n5
Batorska, Janina Wiktoria (née:
    Kucharska), xiii, 93, 94, 95, 96, 97, 98,
    99
Batorska, Krystyna Barbara, Basia, 93, 94,
    97, 98, 99
Batorski, Stanisław, 93, 94, 96, 97, 100n5
Batory, Stefan, 68
Bąk, Franciszek, 85, 87

Bąk, Helena, Hela, 85
Bąk, Jadwiga, Jadzia, 87
Bąk, Katarzyna, Kasia, Murzyczuk, 85, 87
Bąk, Kazimiera, Kazia, 87
Bąk, Marian, 87
Bąk, Marianna, Marynia, 85, 87
Bąk, Marianna (née: Pastuszek), 85, 87
Bąk, Mieczysław, Mietek, 87
Bąk, Stanisław, 85, 87
Bąk, Stefania, 87
Bąk, Waleria. See Sieczka
Bąk, Wanda, Wandzia, 87
Bąk, Władysława, 85, 87
Bąk, Zofia, Zosia, 85
Begin, Menahem, 2
Ben-Elissar, Eliyahu, 2
Beneš, Vojta, 5
Bergman, Blenda. See Boehm
Bergman, Ingrid, 129, 130, 131, 146
Bergman, Justus, 129
Bernadotte, Folke, 53, 57
Bernat, Anna, xv
Bielski, Kazimierz, 18
Boboli, Andrzej, 96, 100n5
Boehm, Carl Norman, 129
Boehm, Blenda (née: Bergman), 129, 131
Boehm, Norman, xv, 36, 37, 82, 129, 131,
    145
Bohdziewicz, Antoni, „Zetka", 58n3
Borczykówna, Danuta, 56
Brandys, Marian, 20

Braun, Sylwester, "Kris", 58n3
Brecht, Bertolt, 105
Brodsky, Josef, 107
Brokaw, Tom, xi
Bronfman, Saidye, 107
Buchanan, Holly, xv
Bulhak, Bohdan, xv, 129
Bulhak, Jan, 129
Bultrowicz, Ewa, 59n17
Bush, George W., 26n12
Bryan, Julian, 45
Brym, Zbigniew, 45
Brzezicka, Barbara, 62, 64, 65, 77, 80
Brzezicka, Elżbieta, 65
Brzezicka, Helena (née: Piwnicka), 62, 83n3
Brzezicka, Lila, 62
Brzezicka, Zofia (née: Weichert), 63
Brzezicki, Bolesław, 62, 83n3
Brzezicki, Eugeniusz, 64
Brzezicki, Mieczysław, 62
Brzezinska, Leonia (née: Roman, 1 voto Żylińska), 2, 8, 25n3
Brzezinski, Adam, 2, 8
Brzezinski, Ian, 25, 26n12
Brzezinski, Kazimierz (Sr.), 25n2
Brzezinski, Kazimierz (Jr.), 25n2
Brzezinski, Lech, 2, 26n12
Brzezinski, Mark, 25, 26n12
Brzezinski, Matthew, 26n12
Brzezinski, Mika, 25, 26n12
Brzezinski, Tadeusz, viii, xii, xv, 1–23, 25n2, 25n3
Brzezinski, Wanda, 26n12
Brzezinski, Zbigniew, viii, xii, xv, 2, 22, 23, 24, 25, 26n12, 74, 82, 84n18

Caldwell, Erskine, 106
Carlyle, Thomas, vii
Caron, Pierre Augustin de Beaumarchais, 110
Carter, Jimmy, viii, xii, 84n18
Cartier, Georges, 13
Chojnacka, Anna, Hanna (née: Chrzanowska, 1 voto: Batkowska), Hania, 46, 48, 58n5
Chopin, Fryderyk, 6, 15–16, 21, 62, 83n4, 83n5, 84n21
Churchill, Winston, xi, 6

Chrzanowska, Halina (née: Borczykówna), Dziusia, xv, 46, 47, 48, 53, 55, 59n18
Chrzanowska, Hanna. *See* Chojnacka
Chrzanowska-Ławniczak, Marta, xv, 58
Chrzanowska, Zofia, 46
Chrzanowski, Jerzy, 46, 53, 58n6
Chrzanowski, Teodor, 46
Chrzanowski, Wiesław, viii, ix, xv, 45, 46, 47, 48, 51, 53, 54, 55, 58, 58n4, 129
Ciołkosz, Adam, 12
Cloud, Stanley, 42
Cody, J.C., 16
Connell, Graham, 122
Copernicus, Nicolaus. *See* Kopernik Mikołaj
Curie, Maria. *See* Maria Skłodowska-Curie
Czerwińska, Halina, Halinka, Zelaźniewicz, 131

Davies, Norman, 82, 84n25
Dragatówna, Hanna, 47
Drew, George, 9
Dubieński, Bernard, 11
Duch, Bolesław Bronisław, 23, 68
Dukszta, Janusz, xv
Dunant, Henry, 67
Dunant, Madame, 67
Dunin-Karwicki, Feliks, 65
Duplessis, Maurice, 16
Dürrenmatt, Friedrich, 109

Eden, Anthony, xi
Eichmann, Adolf, 107
Ensor, David, 82, 84n24

Falkowski, Rudolf. S., viii, xv, 27–38, 41, 43n15
Fiderkiewicz, Albert, 15
Flis, Jesse, xv
Frank, Anne, 107
Frey, James, 127, 128
Frisch, Max, 107

Galloway, Myron, 109
Gawrych, Ludwik, 45
Gem, Pam, 109
Gernand, Agnieszka, xv
Gertler, Władysław, 20
Giedroyc, Jerzy, 34, 35

Gierek, Edward, 31, 42n13
Gilberto, Astrud, 130
Giraudoux, Jean, 107
Glista, Tadeusz, 18
Globenski, Maksymilian, 9
Głogowski, Franciszek, 11
Głuchowski, Janusz, 38
Godbout, Adélard, 6
Goerki, Hans Joachim, 45
Gomułka, Władysław, 31, 42n13
Goodrich, Frances, 107
Gorky, Maxim, Gorki, 136
Grelichowska, Mira, 39
Grimaldi, Giovanni Francesco, 99
Grocholska, Maryjka, Wąsowska, 64
Gruen Victor, 71
Gruszka, Sylwester, 8
Grzedzielski, A.L.M., 5
Guare, John, 109
Gundlach, Jan, 69

Hackett, Albert, 107
Haidasz, Stanley, 9, 11, 33
Halecki, Oskar, 5
Hampton, Christopher, 109
Hamsun, Knut, 136
Hemingway, Ernest, 127, 132
Heydenkorn, Benedykt, 20
Himmler, Heinrich, 53
Hitler, Adolf, xi, 2, 95, 107, 108
Holoubek, Gustaw, 106
Holzer, Jerzy, 36
Hubal, Henryk Dobrzański, 131, 146
Hulanicka, Zofia. *See* Jaroszewicz

Ibsen, Henrik, 109

Jakubowska, Miss, 63
Janaszek-Seydlitz, Maciej, 59n17
Januszewski, Franciszek, 70
Jaracz, Stefan, 112
Jaroszewicz, Amelia (née: Honwalt), 67
Jaroszewicz, Anna, 77, 80
Jaroszewicz, Bolesław, 67
Jaroszewicz, Ewa, 62, 80
Jaroszewicz, Jan, Jaś (Marek's brother),
    62, 65
Jaroszewicz, Jan Marek, Jaś (Marek's son),
    78, 79, 80

Jaroszewicz, Krystyna (née: Brzezicka),
    viii, ix, xv, 61–65, 67, 69–70, 74–75,
    80–82
Jaroszewicz, Marek, viii, ix, xv, 61–62,
    66–74, 76, 79–82, 82n2
Jaroszewicz, Matthew, 80
Jaroszewicz, Stefan, 80
Jaroszewicz, Władysław, 67, 68, 70
Jaroszewicz. Zofia (née Hulanicka), 68
Jaruzelski, Wojciech, 31, 42n13
Jarzebowski, Józef, 98, 100n8
Jasienica, Paweł, 19
Jastrzembski, Oktawian, 16
Jeżewska, Zofia, 62, 83n5
Johansen, Bruce E., xv
Jonas, George, 109
Jones, E. Fay, 62
Jones, Preston, 109
Johnson, Lyndon B., 84n18
Jurczynski, Zbigniew, 17

Kai-shek, Chiang, 97
Kalicka, Janina, Jaroszewicz, 68
Kalkstein, Ludwik, 117
Kareda, Urjo, 109
Kasprzycki Tadeusz Adam, 38
Kelley, Linda, 110
Kierzkowski, Aleksander, Edward, 9
King, Mackenzie, 4
Kleinerman, Samuel, 103
Kopec, Grace, xv
Kopernik, Mikołaj, 6
Korbońska, Zofia (née: Ristau), 61, 80, 82,
    82n1
Korytowski, Zbigniew, 103
Kosciuszko, Tadeusz, 6, 41, 42
Kowal, Antoni, Tony, 90
Kowal, Maria, Marysia, Mary (née:
    Sieczka), viii, ix, xv, 85, 91n1
Kowal Robert Edward, Bob, 90
Kowalska, Faustyna,.Faustina, 98
Kowalski, Frank, 89
Krasicka, Danuta, xv
Krasicki, Janusz, xv
Kraszewski, Charles S., xv, 137n4
Kruczkowski, Leon, 103
Kucharska, Maria, 94, 97
Kulka, Konstanty, 77, 84n21
Kurosad, Jan, 11

La Fontaine, Jean de, 128
Laurent, Louis, St., 7
Łaniewska, Elżbieta, 45
Ławniczak, Anna. *See* Powierża
Ławniczak, Dorota, 53, 58
Ławniczak Grzegorz, 53
Ławniczak, Marta. *See* Chrzanowska
Lechoń, Jan, 120
Le Corbusier (Charles-Edouard Jeanneret), 72
Legge, Bruce J., 137n5
Lelewel, Joachim, 46
Lesage, Jean, 17
Lewenty, Jerzy, 50
Lipski, Józef, 68, 84n19
Lokajski, Eugeniusz, 45
Łopuszański, Tadeusz, 68
Lorentz, Stanisław, 18, 19, 20, 21
Lychowska, Gertruda (née: Seefeld), 117–119
Lychowska, Krystyna (née: Schulz), 122
Łychowski, Tadeusz, 117, 118, 119, 120
Łychowski, Tomasz, viii, x, xv, 117–121
Łyczkowski, Jerzy, 45

Machrowicz, Thaddeus Michael, 74, 84n20
Majewska, Włada, 39
Majski, Ivan, Mayski, viii, xi, 30, 42n3, 95
Maksymowicz, 39
Malatyński, Antoni, 11
Małcużyński, Witold, 16
Malczewski, Zdzisław, 120
Mallett, Gina, 110
Marcinkiewicz, Mariola, xv
Masaryk, Jan, 5
Michalak, Henryk, Henio, 133
Mickiewicz, Adam, 6, 116n1
Miecznikowski, Jerzy, 65
Miller, Arthur, 113
Miłosz, Czesław, 31, 42n12, 63, 83n8
Modzelewski, Karol, 31, 42n12
Mokrzycki, Gustaw Andrzej, 5
Mościcki, Ignacy, 38, 43n16
Mozart, Wolfgang Amadeus, 121
Murzyczuk, Katarzyna. *See* Bąk Katarzyna
Murzyczuk, Wacław, 87, 88

Nagórny, Jerzy, 91n3
Nowicki, Maciej, 68

Odets, Clifford, 109
Olson, Lynne, 42
Olszewski, Tadeusz, „Siwy", 66
O'Neills, Eugene, 106
Ordonówna, Hanka, 28, 42n3
Orłowska, Leontyna, 25n3
Ostrowski, Jan, 11
Ożarek, Henryk, 55

Paderewski, Ignacy Jan, 6, 68, 76, 84n16
Pałaszewska, Mirosława, xv
Palewski, Jean Paul, 21
Paluch, Janusz M., xv
Pavlasek, František, 5
Pawlikowski, Józef, 5
Paz, Octavio, 99
Pearson, Lester, 17
Pease, Neal, xv
Petliura, Symon, 83n15
Piłsudski, Józef, ix, 6, 46, 67, 83n14
Pius XII, 97
Piwnicki, Alojzy, 62
Piwnicki, Marian, 83n3
Plater-Zyberkówna, Cecylia, 63
Podlewski, Stanisław, 54
Polkowski, Józef, 15
Poniatowski, Stanisław August, 19, 21
Poratynski, Jan, 102
Porter, McKenzie, 109
Porwit, Gosia, xv
Potempska, Barbara, 49
Powierża, Anna (née Ławniczak), 53, 58
Powierża, Małgorzata, 59n18
Powierża, Paulina, 58
Prugar-Ketling, Bronisław, 68
Pruszyński, Ksawery, 68
Puacz, Mira, xv
Pula, James S., vii, xv
Pushkin, Alexander, 109

Raczkiewicz, Władysław, 38, 95
Radziwiłł, Family, 25n2
Radziwiłł, Janusz, 91n3
Radziwiłł, Stanisław Albrecht, 98, 100n9
Rayski, Ludomił, 38
Resz, Major, 102
Rittenhouse, Charles, 107
Rodziewicz, Roman, 131, 146
Rodziewiczówna, Maria, 63, 83n6

Roebuck, Arthur, 4
Roman, Antoni, 25n3
Roman, Leon, 25n3
Romer, Tadeusz, 8, 28, 42n5
Romer, Zofia, 28
Ronning Topping, Audrey. *See* Topping
Rossellini, Roberto, 131
Rostworowski, Emanuel, 19
Roth, William V. Jr., 26n12
Roylance, Alla, xv
Rozmarek, Karol, 12
Różycka, Jadwiga, 48
Rube, David, 109
Rueger, Halina, „Małgorzata", 58n3
Rueger, Leszek, „Grzegorz", 58n3

Saarinen, Eero, 70, 71, 84n17
Saarinen, Eliel, 71
Sakiewicz, bombardier, 41
Samardak, Wanda, 119
Sarnecki, Wojtek, 50
Sartre, Jean Paul, 106, 108
Sauve, Paul, 16
Schulz, Anna, 122
Schulz, Jan, 122
Schütz, Alfred, 120
Seneca, 28
Seydlitz, Maciej Janaszek, 59n17
Shakespeare, William, 18, 102, 123
Shamir, Yitzhak, 115
Shaw, Robert, 101, 107, 108
Shellem, Beverly, xv
Slesicki, Tadeusz, 10
Sieczka, Antoni, Antoś, Tony, 86
Sieczka, Helena, Hela, Szoc, 85, 86
Sieczka, Jan, Janek, Johnny, 86
Sieczka, Józef, 85
Sieczka, Katarzyna, Kasia, Lukowska, 85
Sieczka, Ludwik, Louie, 86, 89
Sieczka, Maria. *See* Kowal
Sieczka, Waleria (née: Bąk), 85, 86
Sieczka Władysław, Władzio, 85
Siemaszko, Ewa, 87, 91n5
Siemaszko, Władysław, 87, 91n5
Sienkiewicz, Henryk, 6
Siewierski, Henryk, 120
Sikorski Jerzy, Jurek, „Sikston", 45
Sikorski, Władysław, viii, xi, 6, 30, 32, 34,
  42n3, 95, 100n9, 129

Singer, Isaac B., 136, 137
Siwiec, Jerzy „Jur", 50
Skalski, Stanisław, 31, 42n12
Skłodowska-Curie, Maria, 17, 100n10
Skotnicka, Irena, 45
Skuszanka, Krystyna, 106
Sławoj-Składkowski, Felicjan, 67, 68
Słowacki, Juliusz, 6, 47
Smith, Eberle, 71
Sobieski, Jan, 6
Sommer, Stanisław, 45
Sopoćko, Michał, 98
Sosnkowski, Kazimierz, 6
Spencer, Herbert, vii
Stalin, Joseph, xi, xii, xiiin2, 100n3,
  100n6, 106
Stanisław August. *See* Poniatowski
St.Laurent, Louis, 7, 11
Starostecki, Zdzisław, 133
Stelmaszynski, Wojtek, xv
Styron, William, 22
Strzelecki, Jan, 63
Sulkowski, 68
Sviatopolk-Chetvertynsky, Włodzimierz,
  64, 83n10
Swierz- Zaleski, Stanisław, 15
Synowiec, Joanna (née: Michalak), 133
Szczeniowski, Bolesław, 5
Sznuk, Stefan, 11
Szober, Wincenty, 45
Szylling, Antoni, 8
Szymańska, Cezaria Iljin, "Kaja", 45, 57,
  133, 137n2
Świderski, E., 45
Świderski, Jerzy, 45

Tarnowska, Maria, 64, 83n10
Tarnowski, Adam, 83n10
Tarnowski, Artur, 15
Tatarkiewicz, Władysław, 132
Teitel, Carol, 109
Tenenbaum, Emil, x, 102
Tenenbaum, Hanusia, 102
Tenenbaum, Roza, x, 102, 106
Thompson, Ernest, 109
Thompson, Ewa, xv, 135
Tolstoy, Leo, 136
Tomczyk, Thomas, Tomek, xv, 62, 81
Topping Ronning, Audrey, xv

Tremblay, Michel, 109
Trudeau, Pierre, 17, 18
Tschumi, Jean, 72
Tuwim, Julian, 120
Tyszkiewicz, Michał, 42n3

Uniechowska, Jean, 74

Valentino, Rudolf, 46

Wańkowicz, Krystyna, Krysia, „Anna", 63,
    65
Wańkowicz, Marietta, 63
Wańkowicz, Melchior, xiiin3, 63, 65,
    83n7, 83n12, 128, 135, 137n4, 146
Wańkowicz, Rom, „Knut", 63, 65
Wańkowicz, Witold, 63
Wańkowicz, Zofia (née: Małagowska), 63,
    65
Watt, David Andrew, Jr., 99

Watt, Jadwiga (née: Batorska), 99
Wieczorkiewicz, Maria, 121
Wierzyński, Kazimierz, 120
Williams, Tennessee, 106, 109
Wilson, Woodrow, 84n16
Winfrey, Oprah, 127
Władysiuk, Stefan, xv, 27, 29, 31, 32, 35,
    36, 38
Wojno, Jerzy, 47
Wojtkowski, Tomasz, xv, 130
Wyszyński, Stefan, 14, 16

Zaid, Gabriel, 99
Zamoyski, August, 120
Zawadzki, Stefan, 88
Ziembiński, Zbigniew, 120
Zubrzycki, Angela, xv
Żurakowski, Janusz, 33
Zybała, Stanisław, 53, 59n14
Żyliński, Jerzy, 2, 5

About the Author

Aleksandra Ziolkowska-Boehm, Ph.D. (Warsaw University), an independent scholar, has been the recipient of several awards, including a grant from the Ontario Ministry of Culture, the Institute of International Education, a literature fellowship by the Delaware Division of the Arts, a Fulbright scholarship and a Fulbright award.

Summer 2010. Warsaw Old City Market Square (bombed by Germans after Rising 1944). Photo by Norman Boehm. Archives of Aleksandra Ziolkowska-Boehm.

Among her books are historical biographies, autobiographical stories, a current outlook of Native Americans, and about her beloved feline Suzy.

She is the author of many books published in her native Poland, Canada, and also in the United States, including *"Open Wounds—a Native American Heritage"*; *"On the Road with Suzy: From Cat to Companion"*; *"Kaia, Heroine of the 1944 Warsaw Rising"*; *"The Polish Experience through World War II A Better Day Has Not Come"*; *"Melchior Wańkowicz: Poland's Master of the Written Word"*; *"Fate of a Polish Hero Roman Rodziewicz: Manchuria, Hubal, Auschwitz, Buchenwald, and Postwar Life in England"*; *"Ingrid Bergman and Her American Relatives"*; *"Love for Family, Friends and Books"*.